Leadership in Wonderland

Because sometimes leadership feels like you're falling down the rabbit hole

Happy Reading
Hugs!
Rebecca

Susan Goldberg & Rebecca Lacy

All characters and events portrayed in this publication are fictitious. Any resemblance to real persons, living or dead, is purely coincidental and not intended by the authors.

All rights reserved.
No part of this book may be reproduced, or stored in a retrieval system, or transmitted in any form or by any means, electronic, mechanical, photocopying, recording, or otherwise, without express written permission of the publisher.

Copyright © 2016 Susan Goldberg and Rebecca Lacy
All rights reserved.

ISBN: 10: 1533661960
ISBN-13: 978-1533661968

In celebration of unique leaders everywhere.

CONTENTS

	Introduction	i
	Prologue	iii
1	The Teas	1
2	Dam!	12
3	Dam Interruptions	22
4	Down the Rabbit Hole	30
5	Alice Enters the Darkest Debts	39
6	Unmasking Messes	47
7	A Royal Pain	56
8	Tea Totaling	65
9	Bird Brains	75
10	Beaverly Advice Revisited	85
11	A Smokey Omen	93
11.5	I Spy a Marketing Department	100
12	HR Cawing	108
13	The Truth Revealed	121
14	Fisticuffs: Dueling Potentates	130
15	Gathering Steam	145
16	Leaves of Truth Serum	161
17	The End, the Beginning and the Middle	174
18	Your Story	182

INTRODUCTION

Dear Reader:

Please allow us to introduce you to Leadership in Wonderland. We hope you two will become great friends.

Because you are unique, you will have a singular experience reading the book. Even we, the writers, each learned different things from our characters as they went through their journey.

This book is written to give everyone an individual experience; there aren't any 'prescriptions' – no set lessons of what you are 'supposed to do.' As a result, some will read it as a fun way to pass the time, while others will use it as a guide to help them grow as leaders.

While the book is written as a story, it is filled with personalities and situations common in the real world – some you will recognize, others will be new. Each chapter presents Alice with a new challenge to become more self-aware and confident in her skills as a leader.

At the end of each chapter you will find a corresponding workbook chapter. We encourage you to take time to respond to the questions. There are no right or wrong answers. Rather they are designed to help you reflect upon how Alice's experiences relate to your life.

We can tell you from personal knowledge, discussing the book and workbook is very beneficial. If you have friends or co-workers you can discuss this with, it will deepen your learning experience. You'll discover their decision-making process and insights into the characters and circumstances you may never have considered. It might even change your mind about the way you would have handled a situation.

To access free fillable PDF workbook forms, please visit our website at:

http://www.leadershipinwonderland.com

Finally, if you are using this book to help a child learn leadership lessons or build confidence, it will provide an excellent opportunity for dialogue. Chances are she or he will see things in this book you wouldn't have thought of.

We hope you enjoy accompanying Alice on her odyssey.

Susan Goldberg & Rebecca Lacy

PROLOGUE

It seems a lifetime ago, although it could have happened recently, that Alice encountered a rabbit hole along with a colorful cast of woodland creatures. She was young then. Well, younger than she is today. Since those first introductions, a lot of things have come to pass.

Alice, the curious headstrong adventurer, had an epiphany, although she didn't know it was a brilliant idea at the time. Alice enjoyed the company of her friends from Wonderland. She also loved tea. One day, bored and with nothing to do, Alice thought about starting a game. The game's theme was to develop new tea ideas and sell them. She could play it with her friends. It would be like one big, grown up tea party.

Alice gathered the smartest ones she could find because she wanted it to be a challenging game. She was a smart girl. She explained the theme and the rules and said she wanted to hire them to play different roles, but the roles had to work together in order for the game to succeed. Caterpillar helped the players with the difficult task of choosing their roles, but almost by magic, each player gravitated to a title which would be most suitable for them and their characteristics even without Caterpillar's assistance.

All games become tiresome at some point, and, even more so to children who have yet to master self-control and discipline. After a time, Alice grew weary of the tea "game", although a responsible part of her knew it wasn't a game to the others; after all, she had "hired them" to play their roles. While she was tired of playing an adult businessperson, these folks were taking the game and their roles rather seriously. The others, including Hatter, the Queen, Duchess, Rabbit and Caterpillar would lose their places if she ended the game. Over time, it had become more real and more serious, perhaps that's why it wasn't fun for her anymore, but she didn't want it to end for the others. She didn't want to give up on the tea game; she just didn't want to play anymore.

She thought of an idea that would make them all happy. She spoke with Caterpillar about it because he was the one she trusted most of the group. She told him she wanted to leave the game but she wanted it to continue for the others: Alice wanted Leaves-of-Wonderland to thrive but just not with her playing an active role.

Caterpillar had been advising Alice throughout the game how she could win and then they all could win. Caterpillar explained that with Alice pulling out of the active game board, it left an important place vacant. Together they devised a plan to find someone to take her place but with another additional player to enter into the game, looking out for Alice's best interest so that player would play fair in her place. While she would still have the role of CEO because she had started and organized Leaves-of-Wonderland, Purveyor of Fine Teas, one of the others would take the role of President and the new addition would be Alice's executive assistant.

Alice's first idea was to have Caterpillar play the President but Caterpillar declined, believing he could better serve Alice as a jack of all trades, a fill-in position, as the game progressed, because he was so flexible in his skills. Alice's second choice was less clear, but still logical. Since Hatter had proven himself as a great organizer, planner of tea parties, and obviously had a grand passion for tea, she looked at him as a potential successor for her place in the "game". With Alice and Caterpillar to guide him, when needed, and with the Queen of Hearts, as head of the board of overseers, also managing Hatter, he could wear the hat of President well enough.

Time has passed and the game has blossomed into a legitimate business. Departments have grown, key executives have been added and sales have been very healthy. Since the business, or game in Alice's mind, has been doing well without her guidance and with her assistant in place to report back to her on a regular basis, Alice has allowed the whole thing to progress without her interfering. Caterpillar has since moved on to become an outside consultant because all the key roles of the business have been filled and he can best offer his services on an as needed basis. It has been a dreamy time…until now.

1 THE TEAS

A business can change from a dream into a nightmare in the flash of a smile.

Alice had drifted off to sleep under the leafy oak tree after having a lovely cup of tea. After a time, she had a sense someone else was present. She half-opened one eye and peered out. The first thing that came into focus was Cheshire Cat's grinning whiskered face. She frowned and pouted. "Can't you see I'm busy?" she demanded wearily.

"No," the cat smiled even more broadly, "but I can see you were napping."

"What business is it of yours?" Alice asked crossly.

"It isn't my business, it's yours," he answered without really answering.

"Of course it is my business," she replied then realized there was more he wasn't saying. "But to what are you referring?"

"Your business. It seems while the cat is away there are mice at play."

"You talk in riddles!" she exclaimed. She would love to be rid of the pesky cat, but he was aware of everything everywhere. If he left, he would also take his eyes and ears, which really wasn't at all fair, Alice thought, for it would be so easy for him to leave them behind as he often did when he faded from view. And those eyes and ears were very useful.

"What do you get if you slice a pie in half?" asked the cat.

"What a silly question! Everyone knows you get half a pie," responded Alice peevishly.

"That is what people think, but really you get a whole pie cut down the middle. It isn't until someone eats one half that you have a half remaining."

"I want to go back to sleep now! Please go away and leave me alone!" said Alice laying her head back on her arm in preparation to resume her nap.

Ignoring her demands, Cheshire Cat said, "Hatter is hungry and he wants to eat his half of the pie."

"Then he should," yawned Alice.

"And so he shall . . . .unless, you stop him." taunted the cat, slyly luring the girl back into conversation.

"Why should I stop him from eating his pie, you silly cat?"

"Because the Queen of Hearts is planning on eating the other half. Your half!"

With this Alice bolted up. If there was one thing she simply could not tolerate, it was the Queen of Hearts getting something that was rightfully hers. The thought of the Queen eating her half of the pie made Alice cross, more cross than hot cross buns. Then the girl realized: wait, she didn't have any pie for the Queen to eat. The cat was playing with her, and was evidently enjoying it. This conversation was becoming increasingly infuriating. Lacking the ability to be subtle, she demanded, "Speak to me in plain English, please."

The cat, slowly began to fade from view, leaving only his toothy smile hanging in the air, warning, "If you don't hurry, you will have all the time in the world to dream." Then it, too, silently faded from view.

Alice was still not certain exactly what the cat had meant, but she sensed Hatter and the Queen were up to no good, and whatever they were planning involved taking the pie away from her. That pie was her company, Leaves-of-Wonderland, Purveyor of Fine Teas.

* * * *

Sometime later Cheshire Cat reappeared in front of Alice, startling her. The cat began to tease her with the mention of a foreign threat, one far, far away. Her head spun and worry set in when he further explained that a foreign business was delving into Alice's market and competing with her products directly, even using name brands which resembled hers. That combined with what the cat had described earlier of the two conspirators vying to sabotage her influence and gain control of her company was too much for her. She was raging with disbelief, denial and panic.

Alice seemed a girl of two minds and many doubts, as her head reeled from one thought to another. She talked to herself as she considered her predicament.

"Surely this can't be true, because if it were it would mean I am ignorant, and surely I am not ignorant because I was always told by my mother and sisters how smart I am."

"Why should I believe Cheshire Cat? What does *he* know anyway? He's just a cat. He disappears and reappears so often, how could he know what he's really seen and really heard or just imagined?"

"What does he get out of lying? Perhaps what he's saying is true.

"Wait, if the Cheshire Cat sees this and I don't, how many others are aware of this while I've remained ignorant? What are the others saying? How far have the conspirators gone? How far does their influence go? What's going to become of me and my company?

"I'm just a child, and even though I am a smart girl, should I know all of these things? Am I really ready and equipped to run a company? What was I thinking?"

After a few moments thought, Alice exclaimed, "Hatter may own half the pie, but, but, my half is bigger!" Her confidence was short lived, however. So, it wasn't but the blink of an eye later she once again doubted herself and said, "Still, maybe I shouldn't have given out so much control…but, I don't know everything and I had to bring in experts that did. Yet, did I make the right choices? Did I pick the right characters to run the business? Obviously not, if they are trying to take it away from me. I could say I did nothing to cause this conspiracy, but, obviously I hired selfish characters. Okay, then, I may have made some bad choices but how far do my bad choices go? And what am I going to do about the foreigner problem?" After a moment of thought she continued, "No, never mind the foreign threat, the problem at my doorstep is the one I must address first."

In the midst of her thoughts and worries, Alice was absentmindedly walking. She was so distracted she was unaware of her surroundings and that she had traveled through the woods and into Caterpillar's mushroom lair.

Alice was startled out of her reveries by a voice, which exclaimed, "I say, you seem rather befuddled. What is going on in that mind of yours that you've found yourself at my door?"

"Well…well…well…" She blurted out, "well, I just don't know where to start…"

"Well then, why not start at the beginning."

"I don't know where the beginning is, Caterpillar. Oh, where does it all start?" Alice cried, wringing her hands and then throwing them up in the air in exasperation.

"So then start in the middle." He thought for a second, his hookah in his hand, considered his consulting background, and rephrased what he had meant to say with more clarity, "What is making you so upset, my girl?"

Alice had no time to organize her thoughts. She spoke with raw emotion as she blurted out her story to Caterpillar. She had no time to process the information that was given to her by Cheshire Cat and as a result she seemed a rolling ball of fire with no filter. "I just saw Cheshire Cat. He faded in and out like he always does. Out of nowhere, he starts telling me there's another country producing my teas, or at least a company from that country is producing the teas, my teas, our teas, oh, you know what I mean.

And if that isn't upsetting enough, I have enemies at the company, my own company, our company. They are selfish, greedy characters who want the company for themselves, and are doing this and that to me…and I really don't know what to me. And I don't know what to do. And I don't know what's real, and what's not, or even if the cat is telling me the truth. And I don't know what I don't know and it's all so very confusing and—"

Caterpillar, who always appeared calm, perhaps because of his demeanor in general or possibly because of his fondness for his pipe, was having a difficult time following Alice's rant. Exhaling a giant smoke ring, he interrupted her, saying, "Excuse me, can you please slow down a little? I can't follow you."

"No, I can't! I just can't! Can't you see I am very upset?" Alice calmed herself a little, perhaps conceding that sometimes she does have to slow down to gather her thoughts, and perhaps she should listen more to others. She considered that Caterpillar had worked inside the company as an employee and still works for the company as a consultant. However, she wondered how clear his ideas would be since he always seemed to be so attached to his hookah. She remembered he had been a good friend to her, but he was not privy to everything at the company any more.

"Perhaps, you need to consider things clearly - without so much emotion. You want to have some of my pipe? It might calm you. It seems to help me." He extended his hookah nozzle, offering it to her.

She ignored his kind offer and quickly responded, "How am I supposed to do that? I'm just a child! I'm limited. I don't know what I am supposed to know yet and what I am not. How can I put it all together? I am at a disadvantage."

Adjusting his glasses, Caterpillar thought for a moment while inhaling from his pipe. He was rewarded by a memory of a somewhat similar circumstance from their past. After exhaling a huge wreath of smoke he smiled down at her and said, "Alice, when you were developing the company you were at a similar point to where you are now, and you knew you couldn't do it all by yourself. You couldn't be an expert in everything a company needs, but you were smart enough to know what you wanted to accomplish and also what direction you wanted the company to follow, what your strengths are and also what you weren't capable of giving. So you hired people to help. You now find yourself at a similar juncture again. Carefully consider all of this. You are again in need of outside help."

Alice was still riding a fireball of emotion, and didn't have any patience. Caterpillar's words immediately started to fade as Alice hurried away from him. She simply couldn't listen to anymore of his comments; she was too busy weighing her weighty thoughts in her mind. She knew it was rude of her to leave him in mid-sentence, yet she couldn't listen to him pontificate in consultant's language anymore. After all, who was he to give her advice? However, as she walked along in a fog, his words 'You can't do it all. You need help' played over and over in her mind.

Suddenly, Alice became aware of the sound of bustling activity coming from nearby. The sound grew louder and she looked around to see where it was coming from. She could make it out clearly now. There was splashing mixed with crashing, crunching, and snapping.

Ah, she found it!

A beaver was building a dam in a pond. He was so industrious and steadfast in his activities that Alice became hypnotized by his fluid motions of swimming and placing sticks in a very structured and deliberate manner. She had become so immersed watching the beaver's machinations she hadn't realized her feet were also becoming immersed. She stopped and looked down, finding herself standing in the pond. She swiftly became acutely aware she had cold feet!

WORKBOOK
1 THE TEAS

SUMMARY

Years have passed since the first story of Alice took place. It is somewhat later in time. How much later? Does it matter? Alice, in her later state, is napping, when Cheshire Cat pays her a visit. He explains to her in riddles that Leaves-of-Wonderland: Purveyor of Fine Teas, the company she started earlier in her life, is experiencing problems: The Queen of Hearts and Hatter are plotting against her. In another riddle, the cat leaks to her a foreign entity is an additional threat to her business. Alice questions whether to believe the toothy feline. She also questions if he is telling the truth, does she have the ability to change the situation? Our heroine finds it easier to mull things over while walking, and dreamily walks into Caterpillar's home turf. She mentions her earlier discussions with Cheshire Cat to Caterpillar, once an employee of Leaves-of-Wonderland, now a consultant. As a friend and consultant, Caterpillar tries to offer the founder support and guidance, yet, Alice will have none of it as she is not ready to hear anyone's advice. Further befuddled and emotional, she wanders again, this time becoming easily distracted by a busy beaver's dam building, leaving her vulnerable to further mishaps. This time it's a physical mishap: Alice winds up smack dab in the middle of a stream.

Reminder: Download your free PDF fillable forms at LeadershipInWonderland.com/forms

WHAT ALICE LEARNS

- She has an unrealistic sense of her own abilities and expects herself to be perfect in everything.

- She doesn't know who she is and what she offers.

- When she lets her imagination run away with her, it creates further problems and fears.

What other lessons do you see Alice has encountered in this chapter?

_____

_____

_____

_____

_____

_____

DISCUSSION QUESTIONS

1. Was Alice's nap at the beginning of the chapter symbolic of anything? If yes, what?

What other symbolism or metaphors did you see in the chapter?

2. Alice may doubt her credibility as a CEO and owner, and therefore refers to herself as a "just a child". Have you ever felt like you were an imposter parading like a professional, questioning your own credibility like many leaders have at some point in their lives?

If this has this happened to you, how did you handle the situation?

3. When Alice is told two very negative tales from Cheshire Cat, how can she know whether to trust the Cat? How can she know whether to believe the tales?

SHORT ANSWER QUESTIONS:

1. Rumors/gossip can hurt an organization by: (circle all you feel apply)

   a. Damaging its reputation

   b. Reducing employee morale

   c. Causing employees to question leadership and each other

   d. Damaging trust internally and externally

   e. Creating stress

   f. Producing self-doubt in leaders and employees

   g. Negatively impacting productivity

   h. Costing the organization money

2. Is Cheshire Cat, a....? (circle all you feel apply)

   a. tattle tale

   b. gossip

   c. an ally

   d. nuisance

   e. spy

   f. feline

   g. soothsayer

3. It's difficult for Alice to listen to Caterpillar's advice. Do you feel that's because ...? (circle the best answer).

   a. She believes it's a sign of weakness to need advice

   b. She doesn't fully trust him

   c. She doesn't like him

   d. She judges his dependency on his hookah

   e. He is no longer a full-time employee but an outside consultant

   f. She is still in denial about anything wrong

   Why did you pick this answer?

2 DAM!

"Now look at what you have done!" exclaimed a furious Alice, her hands on her hips, glaring at Beaver. "You have caused me to get cold feet! What do you have to say for yourself?"

"More importantly, why were you not paying more attention? If you had been paying attention to your own business, I can assure you that you would not be standing here with cold feet," Beaver said as he continued to carefully shape a branch to fit the dam he was constructing.

Alice straightened up a bit, considering what he had said. This was something new for Alice. She was accustomed to people giving her their undivided attention; never did they have the impudence to talk back to her. She didn't know what to do about this new development. She certainly didn't want Beaver to know he had left her speechless. So, she simply chose to ignore him as she turned to wade back to the edge of the stream. Having regained her composure, she faced him again, put her little nose up in the air, and tried very hard to sound important. "You should apologize. It was your fault."

"I mind my business; you should mind yours. I'm not going to apologize for you being a silly child. Now, go away. You might not have anything better to do than to play childish games, but I'm very busy."

This truly infuriated Alice and she cried out, "I am not a child! I have not been a child for days and days."

"Then why do you act like one?" Beaver asked.

This gave Alice pause. She crossed her arms and stuck out her lip as she tried to reply to this insulting creature, but she really couldn't come up with anything. Deciding it was better to change the subject, she asked him, "What is the business you are minding?"

At this, Beaver paused in his labors, stood and said with obvious pride, "I build dams."

Alice tilted her dainty head in puzzlement, and inquired, "What is a dam?"

At this question, Beaver ceased his work and stared at her finding it difficult to believe others didn't know what a dam was. "A dam, dear child, is an intricate and deliberate engineering feat."

"Feet?" asked Alice even more puzzled.

Seeing the look on the child's face, Beaver understood immediately her confusion and offered clarification. "Not feet, but *feat*!" Seeing she still wore a look of befuddlement, he continued, "Not the feet like you put in your shoes, but rather F-E-A-T, a spectacular endeavor of unusual skill."

Alice looked closely at the grouping of branches trying to see what made them so special. "It just looks like a bunch of branches piled up in the middle of the stream to me. I don't see why anyone would regard this is as spectacular," Alice responded looking a tad scornful.

"Perhaps to an uneducated eye, it looks like a bunch of branches piled up as you put it. But to the wise, it is much, much more," responded Beaver.

Trying to understand why Beaver was so proud of his silly sticks, she just stared at them, and asked, "Where is the more?"

"The dam holds back water, causing it to be diverted," Beaver answered, his chest puffing out.

"I really don't see why that is very spectacular," she responded.

Once again Beaver paused in his work to look at the impertinent child. Upon further reflection, he recognized even though engineering was his whole world, it was not only possible, but even probable, that she had no previous knowledge of dams. Consequently, it was up to him to help her understand why what he did was so important. With that discovery, he continued with great
patience, "Let me explain: Each component is, by itself, weak. However, when I assemble them in a way that combines their strength they can bring about a tremendous change. No one branch would be able to divert the course of the stream, but together they can. The ability to cause a change is what makes the dam so spectacular."

"Well that is just plain silly," exclaimed Alice. "Who would go to so much trouble to change something?"

Bristling at her insult, Beaver responded, "I would, and so does everyone else who is wise enough to see things aren't as good as they could be."

"Why do things have to change? I don't want to change. I like the way I am."

"Perhaps you do not like change, but change, my dear child, is inevitable. The only question is whether you will cause the change or react to it," Beaver answered her.

Alice thought for the longest time. She stood and thought. She sat on a toadstool and thought. She even laid down in the grass and thought. However, Alice still couldn't quite understand what Beaver had meant. Moreover, being a proud girl, she didn't want to look foolish by asking questions. Instead, she said, "I like the way things are. When you like the way things are, you don't need to change."

Being very wise, Beaver kept his counsel to himself. He knew Alice was just burying her head in the sand, much like Ostrich who lived down the lane.

Beaver's silence bothered Alice. How could she defend her thoughts if he did not respond? "So, you believe I need to change. Is that it?" she demanded, tapping her foot, as though she were looking for an argument. But Beaver certainly didn't have time for an argument.

"Only you can tell you if you need to change," offered Beaver making Alice even more uncomfortable. She was not a girl who wanted to examine herself too closely.

"How do you know something needs to be changed?" she asked. You might consider this question to be of no great importance, but you would be wrong. For by asking this question, Alice admitted that maybe, just maybe there was a slight possibility there were things she didn't know.

"That is a very good question, child. First, you must ask yourself 'Can I imagine something better?' If the answer is yes, then you can begin looking at how things could be better. The changes are how 'better' happens."

"You said the dams cause change. What changes do they make?" Alice asked in a voice that sounded like a challenge. She still didn't really understand his meaning, but wasn't quite ready to admit to

Beaver or to herself that she had some things to learn.

The puzzled look on the girl's face made him realize he needed to give her examples to help her to see what he meant. "I change the trees by cutting them down and stripping the leaves so each piece fits together so the whole structure is strong. This will allow the pieces to work together as a dam. The dam changes the course of the stream. This creates a splendid wetland, which is home to many creatures. Some people would like for things to stay the same, so they don't like what I do. For others, however, the changes are very important."

Alice rested her chin on her fist. This new information about change was something she needed to ponder. After a bit, an idea popped into her head. "Just because it is your business to change things, doesn't mean it's *my* business." This seemed to make her feel much better. She still wasn't comfortable with the idea of associating too closely with change.

Beaver paused in his work to study her. "Your business is to be a child, to learn and to grow. That is the very heart of change. It isn't something to be feared, but rather to be embraced. It is something to look forward to like a big birthday present."

"I don't know that growing up is such a big birthday present," she said with a note of sadness in her voice. "I've been forced to grow up way too soon, dealing with an unpleasant situation that has just appeared on my doorstep. That is how my feet ended up in your stream."

Puzzled, Beaver asked in a kindly voice, "My dear, where was your head when you got cold feet earlier?"

Alice didn't expect that question. She thought Beaver was going to tell her she had to change. Grownups are always telling us what we need to do. She pondered his question and finally answered, "I got cold feet because I was in a hurry."

"Go on," encouraged Beaver.

"Well, I was in a hurry to get away from my business because…"

Beaver interrupted. "Excuse me? Your business?"

"Oh yes," she replied. "My business, you know, Leaves-of-Wonderland: Purveyor of Fine Teas. Anyway, people were saying terrible things—"

Again Beaver couldn't help but interrupt Alice as he tried to digest this new information, which was tougher than any wood he had ever chewed. "You say you have a business? But you are just a child! How can you possibly have a business?"

Alice sighed deeply. How could she recount her tale so Beaver would understand? "I have a business I started long ago. It was like a make-believe game to me. Suddenly, I found it was real and there were things I needed to know in the real world I didn't need to know in a make-believe one."

"Go on," encouraged Beaver when Alice paused to gather her thoughts.

"It all started because I was playing tea party. That grew and grew into a real company – Leaves-of-Wonderland. Now it's not my old playmate friends gathered around the table, sipping my tea and chatting about pleasant things. Now there are cruel people who want to take my company away. There are even people in a far off land I used to imagine was make-believe who want to steal my recipes." Alice took a breath and continued.

"I was looking to escape from the terrible things people have recently told me. You see, once the tea party started turning into less of a party and more of something serious, I left it to look for a new game. I left Leaves-of-Wonderland for someone else to play with, but I didn't give it to him! I was just told by an unbiased feline source that person and another important person may be up to no good. That same cat told me about my foreign competition.

"After leaving Leaves-of-Wonderland for so long, I am at a loss as to what to do to get back into the party. Beaver, I don't know what I don't know. Furthermore, my feline friend said some very sneaky people are saying terrible things about me. I couldn't bear to hear anymore and needed some time to clear my head. When I saw you busy with your business, my attention was drawn away from those unpleasant thoughts and I got off track, ended up standing here with cold feet." This admission by Alice left her feeling spent - she needed to rest. It wasn't easy to admit those kinds of things.

"Are your feet feeling any warmer now?"

"Why, yes they are," Alice replied. "But I still don't want to hear the terrible things Cheshire Cat and Caterpillar were saying. It made me feel all anxious inside."

Beaver processed this information Alice had shared. He asked her, "Would you like to be able to listen to them and not feel anxious?"

"No. I just want them not to tell me things I don't want to

hear!" she yelled, punctuating her response by stomping her foot in its patent leather Mary Jane.

"I see. You would rather they keep secrets from you, even if the information is for your own good?"

This was something Alice had not considered, and now that she was considering it, it made her head hurt. "No, I suppose I don't want that either."

"Perhaps you would like to learn how to mind your own business and feel better about all the troublesome issues that arise," Beaver offered.

"Oh, yes, I would like that very much." Alice exclaimed, clapping her hands in excitement. Suddenly, she stopped and a frown creased her brow. "Does this mean I have to change?"

"Everything changes, dear girl, even the hardest stone changes with the forces of nature and time. Without change, nothing ever gets better," Beaver assured her.

"But I don't know how. How can I change if I don't know how?" Beaver gnawed on a piece of wood as he watched Alice mull this over in her mind. He paused, giving the matter great consideration. Finally, he replied, "It won't be easy." Seeing this didn't dissuade her, he continued, "Sometimes you might have to do things that are uncomfortable." She nodded her understanding, and he added, "I will help you, but mostly, you have to help yourself. It will be an adventure!"

And with that, Alice stepped out of the water and into a journey, which would enlighten, brighten, and sometimes frighten her.

WORKBOOK
2 DAM!

SUMMARY

Alice finds herself standing in the stream and in a foul mood because she has been distracted by Beaver's dam building. Unwilling to accept responsibility for her current situation, she shifts the blame to him. When Beaver does not apologize for her soggy shoes, Alice is stunned because she is unaccustomed to people pointing out her bad behavior. Her anger is soon replaced by curiosity about the industrious Beaver's activities. When Alice asks him what he is doing, Beaver explains his business is to build dams, and the reason he does this is to cause change. Seeing the puzzled look on Alice's face, he goes on to explain that change is necessary to make things better. Alice is appalled. She is quite certain she doesn't like change. Change causes uncertainty, and to Alice, admitting change is needed is the same as admitting things aren't good enough, and she takes this quite personally. However, after some further inquiry, Alice begins to see that, perhaps, change may be a good thing. By the end of their initial conversation, Alice has begun to recognize she is going to have to make some changes in order for her company to survive. She even admits she might need some assistance, and asks Beaver to help her.

WHAT ALICE LEARNS

- Being presented with any news, be it good or bad, is better than having it withheld.

- Change is necessary for growth.

- It is okay to admit your shortcomings and ask for assistance.

What other lessons do you see Alice has encountered in this chapter?

_____
_____
_____
_____
_____

DISCUSSION QUESTIONS

1. Alice approaches Beaver in a very negative manner, and his first reaction is to respond to her in the same way. If someone approaches you in a way you don't like, how do you ensure you don't cause the situation to escalate by responding back in the same manner?

2. Many people think a leader is required to have all the answers. In fact, it is more important to know the right questions to ask, and of whom to ask them. How would you advise Alice to use this leadership technique to enhance her rapport with Beaver?

3. Initially Alice sees change as a major threat. She may even see it as a sign of weakness to admit change is necessary. She certainly does not welcome it.

What about change bothers you most?

What about change do you most welcome?

How does your outlook on change have an impact on your life?

SHORT ANWER QUESTIONS

1. On a scale of 1 to 10 (with 1 being worst and 10 being best) how would you rate your ability to adapt to change? _____

2. At the beginning of the chapter, Alice is quite snippy. In fact, she is in a foul mood. Why is this so? Is it because… ? (Circle all that apply)

    a. her feet are wet

    b. Beaver saw her make a mistake

    c. she's hungry and needs a Snickers

    d. she realizes she isn't perfect

    e. there are threats to her company and she had been unaware of them

    f. she realizes she is the problem

    g. because she is a moody person

    h. Other: _____

3. Alice has demonstrated she does not want to hear bad news even at the expense of her company. Have you ever avoided a situation when you knew you were going to be confronted with bad news?

    Yes____   No_____

3 DAM INTERRUPTIONS

As she was having the intense conversation with Beaver, which would herald the beginning of a new chapter for Alice, in the back of her mind she heard a patter of steps becoming louder and louder. She tried to disregard it for fear it would bring more unwanted news, but then there came a voice. "Alice, Alice" it called. The voice became shriller and increasingly desperate. She paid no attention to the voice, commanding herself to pay attention to Beaver instead. But when she felt a tap-tap of a flipper on her shoulder, she could no longer ignore the presence.

She turned around. A small bespectacled penguin stood on a large toadstool. "Alice, stop ignoring me. You know you can't do this for long. You're ignoring me just like you ignore things at the company when you don't want to deal with them. Stop this behavior. Clearly, it doesn't work to your benefit!"

Alice looked down at her assistant, Penguin, and shook her head. "What are you talking about, Penguin? Can't whatever you have to say, wait? You're being very rude."

"Rude? Rude? We don't have time for pleasantries and polite conversation right now, Missy. There's something strangely amiss at the company and I am trying to gather clues as to what is going on and it needs your attention."

Alice knew when Penguin used the name "Missy", he wasn't mincing his words. So she stopped to listen to what he had to say. "Please excuse me, Beaver, my assistant, Penguin, needs my attention, apparently very badly. In fact, badly enough to interrupt me," she said as she turned to Penguin with a stern expression. "Go on, Penguin."

"I've noticed everybody is acting very strangely and it's been going on for quite some time. But now I realize it's throughout the company except for perhaps you and me...and maybe Caterpillar because he is not involved with day to day operations anymore and is apart from the rest of the team."

"What are you saying, Penguin?" Alice asked dismissively, sounding like one of her sourly board members, The Queen of Hearts.

"I don't really know what I am saying other than something is very amiss and we need to get to the bottom of this. I have heard rumblings when I've found myself around the Hatter's office. "

Trying to sound mature and commanding in front of Beaver and yet truly innocent and unaware of things like corporate espionage, Alice admonished Penguin. "When you've found yourself around Hatter's office? Listen to you, Penguin, are you spying on the Hatter? Is that polite?"

"What else can I do? I have to be YOUR eyes and ears and gather information for you because YOU are not paying attention. I don't have a choice and the way things are going YOU don't either." The penguin realized he had been shouting and politely lowered his voice a few notches when he made the following statement, "Because if you don't, you are going to find yourself without a company. As it is, the staff's loyalty to you is fading fast, and your behavior is not helping matters".

Alice stared at the penguin like she had just seen him for the very first time. She was amazed and quite dazed by his strong words and scolding tone, but she was touched by his loyalty. "You, you, never listen except when you want to, when everything is going your way - when you're told what you want to hear. Not this time, Alice. This time you are going to listen because you have to! Your company depends on it. And you love your company and deep down you have loyalty to your employees. Perhaps it's time to grow up and get your head out of the tea leaves."

The caterpillar's words came back to Alice. "You can't do it on your own. You need help." Caterpillar may be in his own fog of smoke, but he was right, and Alice recognized Penguin was one of those who could help her.

"Come, Alice", said the Penguin. "Let's go figure this out together before things get any worse". Penguin jumped down from the toadstool and waited for Alice to follow him.

"Well", she thought, "if I have to head into troubled waters and unchartered territories, I might at least take someone with me who can help me see and do what needs to be done and wants to support me". He could help her make some sense of things. And unlike Caterpillar, he was not a habitual smoker, nor was he someone who appeared and disappeared at his own will like Cheshire Cat. No, in Alice's mind there was no comparison, Penguin was steadfast and diligent.

Realizing it was important for Penguin to have all the information, Alice confided the rest of what she had learned from Cheshire Cat and Caterpillar. "Penguin, did you know *Eastshire* is imitating our teas with similar brand names? Yes, someone there is practically trying to steal our identity. And the strangeness you have witnessed at the company goes along with Cheshire Cat's tales of conspirators within our midst! He told me he heard talk of two conspirators at the company who are trying to wreak havoc".

At this news, Penguin exclaimed, "Then, it's even more important we begin our investigation immediately".

"Penguin, if we investigate, what will we find? Will we find something that will cause me to change in any way? And, and, do you think I can change? Beaver tells me I must change if my business is to change."

"Beaver? Who is Beaver to all this? What does he know?" asked a confused Penguin as Alice smiled apologetically at Beaver for her assistant's dismissive comment. "Alice, I don't know what you and I will find, but together, we can get results. I know we can. I know we will!" Of that, Penguin was sure.

Alice liked his optimism. Perhaps she could catch it? And her thoughts about Beaver's teachings? That could wait for another time. Right now called for observation so she knew what she had to change in the future. Alice was drawn back into her own immediate reality and away from Beaver's broader lessons. Perhaps she would learn those lessons by confronting her problems.

WORKBOOK
3 DAM INTERRUPTIONS

SUMMARY

While Alice is in the midst of a lesson from Beaver, she is rudely and determinedly interrupted by her assistant, the dapper Penguin. She tries to ignore him; however, he has an important agenda: her business is in turmoil for many reasons and Penguin wants to understand why and then help her fix it. He would like Alice to regain her interest in her company and goads her into demonstrating she really does care for Leaves-of-Wonderland. Alice realizes she does care to the extent she would like to investigate along with Penguin's help all the potential troubles within the company. She realizes she can't do it alone and Penguin has shown himself through the years to be loyal, hardworking and smart. Most importantly, she knows she can trust him. For the meantime, Alice tables the changing she must eventually do in order to grow while the two companions investigate the entire situation at Leaves-of-Wonderland. The journey through the company's nooks and crannies is about to begin.

WHAT ALICE LEARNS

- She needs to do a better job of recognizing the good qualities and attributes of others.
- She needs to learn patience.
- She needs to be more receptive to information people bring to her.

What other lessons do you see Alice has encountered in this chapter?

_____

_____

_____

_____

_____

_____

DISCUSSION QUESTIONS

1. Alice is under the misconception that if she hired the right people the company should operate successfully without any of her further supervision or feedback. Why is feedback so important?

2. Alice's feelings of superiority have shown up again and again in how she treats others, from Caterpillar to Beaver to Penguin. It is assumed she is entitled to her reactions because she is the founder and CEO of the business. How do you feel people respond to a leader who exhibits an attitude of superiority?

3. Alice seems unaware of who she is, including her weaknesses. Caterpillar, Beaver and Penguin have all tried to politely enlighten Alice so she can better understand herself and her motivation. She prefers to ignore their comments.

   What do you see as her weaknesses?

   Why is it important to understand your weaknesses as a leader?

   What can you do about them?

   Who is the appropriate individual to provide guidance to a leader?

   Why?

SHORT ANSWER QUESTIONS

1. Alice, like many people, is impatient. What she doesn't realize is that the more impatient she is the more others will respond to her in a negative way. What kind of behavior can she expect from others when they are responding to her impatience?

    a. they ignore her

    b. they keep silent, because they are afraid to speak

    c. they withhold information

    d. they pushback with anger

    e. they give her lip service but do what they want

    f. all the above

2. Alice has chosen to be blind to many things. Which of the things below has she actually been aware of?

    a. Her mistreatment of others

    b. She has left the company to its own management for far too long

    c. Her attention can be diverted easily

    d. She doesn't enjoy listening to others particularly when they are telling her she is mistaken

    e. She is having conversations with animals

    f. She is not yet aware of any of these things

    Why did you pick this answer?

3. Alice cannot expect Leaves-of-Wonderland to thrive until she can confront her own weaknesses.

   True or False?

   Why do you feel that way?

4 DOWN THE RABBIT HOLE

Alice excused herself from Beaver's presence. "Excuse me, dear Beaver, but Penguin needs me".

"The company needs you" corrected Penguin.

By this time Beaver had already gone back to his work, having been ignored for the better part of the entire conversation between Alice and Penguin. Alice hadn't even noticed Beaver had finished with her and had turned to his branches again. She had been very rude, but Beaver realized she had important business to take care of, and, therefore, had excused her behavior. She was a child, after all. He couldn't hold her to adult expectations.

"Where are we going, Penguin?" She asked as she followed the waddling figure.

"Why, we are going where we should, to visit all the nooks and crannies of Leaves-of-Wonderland. We are going to every area of the company so we can see what is going on with our own two eyes, uh, our own four eyes, yours and mine." The black and white body bounced forward quickly, and Alice could barely keep up even though her legs were much longer and she was so much bigger than Penguin.

"But I've never gone to visit all the areas of the company before. The department heads know how to lead their departments well enough. I trust they can run things. They don't want me checking in on them. After all, how would that look? It would look like I don't trust them. That's what it would look like. Can you imagine a founder of a company who doesn't trust her people and how they operate? Can you imagine what they will all do when they see me?" Alice wasn't sure if she was trying to convince Penguin what they were doing was wrong or herself, but Penguin was not budging from his original plan. He was very stubborn, and Alice could do nothing but mumble incessantly, trying to stop their progress.

Penguin halted abruptly. He looked at Alice as sternly as he could and barked, "Are you done? You are the founder of a company. All founders who own the majority stakes of a company - and may I remind you, you do own 51% of the business - all founders oversee in some way all, the entire all, of the facets of their company. And you, Missy, have not been doing that. Gosh only knows what is happening at this company now because you have not performed your responsibility of regular visits with your staff. I can only hope we get there in time to save the company; that we can stop the madness that has spread".

Alice was shocked by the Penguin's harsh tone, in fact, it scared her. With tears in her eyes, she started to shake and blurted out, "B-b-but, what madness? Penguin, you are scaring me. Of what do you speak?"

Penguin took out the pocket handkerchief he always carried, being the dapper fellow that he is, and gave it to Alice to dry her eyes. His tone softened, "Now, Alice, we don't know anything yet. I am sorry to upset you so, but we are going to find out."

With her tears dried, Alice pulled herself together. She admitted to Penguin and to herself that she was scared. She was plenty scared of a lot, and she felt she had good reason to be. "Penguin, if I visit and talk to all the staff in their departments, I will see how much I don't understand about the company. I will see how ignorant I am of everything I've chosen not to learn. And worse, they will see how ignorant I am. They will lose confidence in me and I will lose what little confidence I have in myself".

Penguin gently brushed the leg of the girl. He had more confidence in her than she did. He knew what she was capable of. "There, there, Alice. There's no time like the present to start learning, right? And you can ask questions, you are good at that, and they can teach you enough so you can understand it all".

Alice wondered whether she needed the help of someone like Beaver to understand all the departments truly as she should, or Caterpillar or Cheshire Cat, but she gathered her confidence and decided to push forward with Penguin.

"First stop is Rabbit's house. In a manner of speaking, Operations is his kingdom. A kingdom ruled largely by the pocket watch that is as much a part of Rabbit as his ears", Penguin announced to Alice. The two walked until they came to Rabbit's realm. Without so much as a knock, Penguin pushed open the wooden door.

Rabbit, alarmed, quickly hopped up from his chair and turned towards the trespassers, his body shaking. "Oh, oh, this simply won't do! What are you doing here? No, no, can't you see you are going to interrupt my flow of paperwork and that can't be permitted. I am on a strict time-table. You are confusing me! You are not welcome here. Who invited you? You are in my domain. I don't remember sending an invitation for you to join me in my office. No, no, you do not belong here. Go away." Rabbit barely took a breath between each statement and was quite dizzy when he was done with his diatribe.

Penguin and Alice moved toward the nervous Rabbit. Penguin approached him with an air of authority, while Alice lagged behind moving carefully so as not to frighten Rabbit any more than he already was. "Rabbit", explained Penguin simply, "Alice is the founder of this company. She is the majority owner. She doesn't need an invitation to come visit you. In fact, she has an open invitation."

"Well, that's simply not fair. That's not fair at all." Rabbit blurted. He couldn't take the time to determine whether it was fair or not, that would take too much time away from his precious schedule. Frankly, fairness didn't matter to him: only time did. That and his privacy.

He stood cross-limbed in front of his beloved table, which served as his desk, guarding his work and bolstering his confidence. He was territorial, not because he felt he had something to hide from the founder of the company, but because he had no time to prepare for her visit. He had no time to tidy up and no time for niceties. Rabbit was keenly aware of the precious time that was ticking away and he had deadlines.

While Rabbit had his eye on Penguin, who was the more confrontational of the two, Alice slid around Rabbit and Penguin. She stepped up to the table Rabbit was working from, and peered over his shoulder. She realized she was curious about what Rabbit was doing. She wanted to know. She started moving papers that were on the desk so she could read them closely. She glanced at one page, then another, and then yet another. Her brow wrinkled. "Rabbit, what on Earth are you doing here? It seems you are very busy, but the information on these papers doesn't seem to be going anywhere. What are you supposed to be doing?"

"I am very busy. I don't have time to explain things to you! I am busy, busy, busy! I have an important job here. Without me, nothing at Leaves-of-Wonderland operates like it should."

She turned to her assistant. "Penguin, it does seem that Rabbit is very busy, but I am not sure what he is busy about. Look at this paper. Even I can see that these calculations don't make sense. There are problems here. And it looks like Operations is not operating very well at all."

Penguin jumped on a nearby ottoman and asked Alice to bring it closer to him. He grabbed the papers Alice had been reading with his flippers and rustled through them quickly. "Well I am not an owner here, and I do not have your training, Alice, but I dare say you are right. Some of this does not make sense. Look at manufacturing. Look at marketing . . ."

Rabbit hastily pulled the papers away from the busybody twosome. "Let me get back to work. I must do this quickly or Hatter will not be happy." And then he muttered "And if you do not like my work, simply say so and then leave. You will not force me to be late." Rabbit harrumphed. He was fiercely protective of his work as he cared deeply about getting things done.

"Rabbit", Alice started carefully because she realized she had been rude and accusatory. "These calculations per department don't make sense. Maybe you could explain them to me so I might understand them better?"

"Explain them to you? Explain them to you! No, I can't. I've done nothing wrong. If there are any problems here it's because of the finance department. They gave me these numbers to work with. It's their fault. It's their mess, not mine".

Alice was uncertain whether Rabbit was just shifting the blame to an innocent party or whether he was right. However, she realized she had been too hasty and was willing to give Rabbit the benefit of the doubt. She knew her next step would be to visit the finance department to see if she could corroborate Rabbit's story. "Come, Penguin," and she helped her small assistant off the ottoman, "let's visit Finance and see if we can learn more".

Penguin stepped off the ottoman with the help of Alice's outstretched arm, marveling at the change in his young leader, especially in the last few minutes. He thought, "She does care. She is curious. She wants to make things right. And she is listening. In this case, her curiosity is a good thing. It is making her grow and take responsibility. Alice can be the leader I know her to be." The small creature tried to hide his inner glee so as not to alarm Alice or call attention to her behavior, which could make her self-conscious or worse stall her momentum. He happily waddled behind her as they left the environs of Rabbit's lair.

WORKBOOK
4 DOWN THE RABBIT HOLE

SUMMARY

With Penguin's less than gentle prodding, Alice begins her quest to find out what is happening at Leaves-of-Wonderland. Taking the first step causes her quite a bit of trepidation as she fears that by going to visit the various departments, she is communicating both her lack of trust in the managers' abilities as well as her own lack of knowledge about what is happening within her company.

The twosome makes their way to the first stop: Operations, which Rabbit governs with strict adherence to schedule. Rabbit is insulted when Alice and Penguin dare to disrupt his routine, and he does nothing to hide his displeasure. While Rabbit is trying to convince Alice and Penguin to leave so he can get back to his timetable, Alice catches a glimpse of some papers, containing a lot of figures, which cause her to question what Rabbit is so busy doing. She challenges him by saying the figures on the papers don't make sense. At that, Rabbit becomes increasingly defensive, and Alice quickly realizes her tactic is not going to help her gain any useful information to continue her quest. In fact, it might prove to be counterproductive. Changing strategies, she asks for Rabbit's assistance to understand the content of the papers. Rabbit's explanation is quick to accuse the finance department for having created the mess, which resulted in the questionable figures. Alice recognizes this might simply be a ploy to get rid of her and place the blame on another department, but she is willing to investigate further in order to discover the truth.

WHAT ALICE LEARNS

- Honey attracts more bees than vinegar.
- The ability to communicate effectively is a sign of strength.
- As owner, she has the right and responsibility to ask hard questions and expect answers.

What other lessons do you see Alice has encountered in this chapter?

_____
_____
_____
_____
_____
_____

DISCUSSION QUESTIONS

1. There seems to have been a lot of tension in the discussions with Rabbit. How could Alice have better diffused the situation with Rabbit so she might have received better cooperation?

2. What signs should Alice look for to determine if an employee, like Rabbit, is genuinely busy or just "busy being busy" as she accused him of being?

3. If you were in Rabbit's situation, what would you be assuming and feeling about your leader after Alice's visit? What questions would you have had for Alice?

SHORT ANSWER QUESTIONS

1. Asking questions is a sign of

   a. Strength _____
   b. Weakness _____

   Why did you answer as you did?

4. What might Rabbit be trying to hide?

   a. The figures on the papers on his desk
   b. He isn't accomplishing anything
   c. His cluttered desk
   d. His love of timepieces
   e. That he spent too much on his Rolex pocket watch

   Why did you select the answer you chose?

5. If Alice wants to work together with Rabbit, what does she have to do? (circle all that apply)

   a. Convince Rabbit they are both working for the good of the company
   b. Show him her watch collection
   c. Make him clean off his desk
   d. Threaten to fire him if he doesn't become more organized
   e. Compliment his commitment to timeliness

   Why did you choose that/those answers? How will those actions assist Alice?

5 ALICE ENTERS THE DARKEST DEBTS

As the duo walked down the path, it gradually morphed from a lovely garden scene into a forest of frightening trees, which resembled steel cabinets. The colors, which were once so pleasing, now faded to black and white with only the occasional red line Alice was certain no one would dare cross.

"My, this is a frightening place." she said in a hushed tone. Beside her she could feel Penguin trembling. In spite of their trepidation, they continued on knowing the only way to get to the bottom of the problem was to face their fears.

When Alice and Penguin had at last reached the finance department, they stepped through the door. Everything was very, very quiet as though they were all playing hide and seek. Not a creature could be heard, except for a tiny mouse who said, "Why are you here?"

"I'm sorry to disturb you," replied Alice.

"Yes, yes, yes, that's all well and good, but can't you see we are very busy?" demanded Mouse.

"It's just that we went to speak with Rabbit, and he said the problems with Operations are all your fault." Penguin hung his head a bit, realizing too late that he had started on the wrong foot.

"What a lot of falderal!" exclaimed Mouse in a voice that was as forceful as his diminutive size would allow. "Just who are you to come in here and question our professionalism?"

"Why, I'm Alice. Don't you recognize me?" she asked incredulously.

Mouse became terribly distraught at Alice's words. "Is this some kind of a trap?" he demanded. "My lineage is of those who are not fond of traps."

"Oh, no," exclaimed Alice. "It's no trap. I *really* am Alice, the founder of the company, and Rabbit did say we are in a terrible mess, and I need you to fix it."

"If a mess there is, I can assure you it was not created by the finance department," Mouse attested haughtily.

"How can you be sure since I haven't even told you what it is?" asked a perplexed Alice.

Mouse, who was never one who took well to being doubted, bristled and frowned, his ears turning red. "It doesn't matter what it is, I am sure that the finance department simply cannot be blamed for it."

By this time the rest of the department had gathered around to see what the racket was all about. Surely it must be something terrible to cause Mouse to roar in such a manner.

"What is this all about?" demanded the department's manager, Dodo.

"Perhaps," offered Penguin "if you tell him what you require, Dodo will be able to assist you."

"I need you to help clean up your mess," stated Alice wondering why she needed to repeat this.

"There is no mess," Dodo assured her. "Your finances are in perfect condition."

Alice had a puzzled look on her face as she asked him, "Are you sure?"

"Certainly I'm sure or I wouldn't have said so," exclaimed Dodo. "If you want me to give you an in-depth analysis, I will be happy to. You just give it to me, and then I will give it to you."

"I don't understand," Alice said, tilting her head as she pondered what he said.

"It is a fiduciary matter. It requires reciprocity of transactions. First, you must give it to me."

"What is 'it'?" asked the befuddled Alice.

"'It' is typically something you have lost," announced Duck, who was a very helpful clerk in the finance department.

"But I haven't lost anything," cried Alice.

"Ah, see everything is fixed now," responded Mouse in a self-satisfied fashion.

Alice started to say that everything was not fixed when she was interrupted by Lory who said deridingly, "I am much older and wiser than you. I say it is fixed, thus it is." With that, he glared at her, challenging Alice to disagree.

"I don't know that you are much older, and I don't know what that has to do with this matter. I just know it hasn't been cleared up."

Mouse was insulted at being challenged. Dodo looked anxious. Why couldn't she just take their word for it and go away? Lory looked angry having had his age and wisdom challenged. Duck looked hopeful that perhaps this situation might really be cleaned up soon.

This wasn't going as Alice had hoped it would. Then Eaglet, the other member of the finance department, spoke up. "Perhaps you could explain what you and Rabbit think the mess is. If we understand it better, maybe we can help you know who to talk to and how to clean it up." Penguin breathed a sigh of relief that here, at last, was someone who might be able to make sense of this madness.

Alice didn't know what to say. She thought to herself, "Why should I explain? Since it is a problem they created, why don't they just fix it?" Sensing Alice was about to say something she ought not, Penguin tapped the back of her leg with his flipper. Understanding his meaning, Alice thought again and realized that maybe what Eaglet had said was right. 'Maybe', she thought, 'if I share information with them, it will be easier for them to help me.' Then she had another great big thought that was so big, it made her eyes open very wide. 'Maybe,' she thought, 'if I listened better, people would tell me more.'

With these thoughts in mind Alice sat down with the finance department and talked finance. Alice found that when she asked questions in a tone that didn't sound like she was accusing them, they were more than willing to supply the answers…sometimes they even answered questions Alice didn't know enough to ask. All in all, it was a very fulfilling experience for her.

In spite of the success Alice felt she'd had in Finance, she realized she still didn't have all the information needed to clean up the mess. For instance, Finance seemed to function well enough and the team seemed responsible, but Operation's figures were wrong. What was Rabbit doing with them? Was he the guilty party or was he just one of the many problems?

She admitted to herself that in order to get the answers to these questions, she must continue her quest. The next leg of their journey was Manufacturing. There she would gain additional knowledge which would help her to have a better understanding of what she had learned in Operations and Finance. Once they visited Manufacturing, Alice hoped all the pieces of the puzzle would fall together neatly so she would have a clear picture of Leaves-of-Wonderland.

WORKBOOK
5   ALICE ENTERS THE DARKEST DEBTS

SUMMARY

    Alice and Penguin leave Rabbit's lair with a whole lot of questions, which lead them away from the garden path to a vision devoid of color where everything is black or white. Their new surroundings are frighteningly stark and leave no room for middle ground: they have entered the world of the finance department.

    Mouse meets them at the department door desiring to know who they are and what they want from his department. Alice explains they had just met with Rabbit in the operations department and were disconcerted by the paperwork on his desk, which pointed to the absolute mess Leaves-of-Wonderland had become operationally. They went on to explain that Rabbit claimed the mess originated in the finance department. Therefore, Alice, as the owner of the company, must investigate his claim.

    Mouse, is incensed by the accusations of Rabbit and Alice, and raises his voice to demonstrate his displeasure. The rest of the department in hearing the distress of their colleague, Dodo (department manager), Duck, Lory, and Eaglet comes to the mouse's defense. A sharp dialogue ensues between Alice and the finance group until she realizes blaming others without listening to their side of the argument is not fair.

    She and Penguin sit down with the Finance folks and talk finance until she feels comfortable all her questions have been asked of this one department. Yet, riddles and puzzles remain; Alice and Penguin still do not have all the answers. While the owner of the company feels wonderfully satisfied about controlling her frustration and listening calmly to the noisy bunch, which is a great feat for her, Alice understands she and Penguin must continue to venture onward to visit still another department hoping to gather additional information.

    Next stop: Manufacturing

WHAT ALICE LEARNS

- Alice is seeing that things aren't always simple: issues in business are not always black or white; they can be gray.
- By asking questions and listening one can build rapport and understanding, which opens the opportunity for cooperation.
- Alice sees a team who works well together is supportive of each other.

  What other lessons do you see Alice has encountered in this chapter?

  _____
  _____
  _____
  _____
  _____

DISCUSSION QUESTIONS

1. Mouse's behavior at the outset of the chapter was very strong for such a little animal. How would you feel if someone questioned your professionalism? Is there a better way Alice could have handled herself with Mouse and still have been able to receive the answers she wanted from him and his finance colleagues?

2. What were some of the positive traits the department exhibited during Alice's visit she should have considered in her discussions with them?

3. When did Alice have an "about face" during this chapter? What do you suppose triggered the change in her behavior?

SHORT ANSWER QUESTIONS

1. Which best describes the finance department? (Circle one answer you feel is the best)

- a. They are a bunch of bird brains
- b. They are an argumentative group
- c. The team believes they have done the best job with the financial statements given the resources and information provided to them
- d. They are uncooperative
- e. They are overly defensive in their combined attitude.

   Why did you select this answer?

6. In your opinion, at the close of the chapter, did it seem Rabbit was justified in offering up the finance department as the culprit of the company's problems?

    True   False

    Why did you select this answer?

7. Alice should have conferred with Dodo, the finance department manager, if she had concerns, rather than addressing Mouse.

    True   False

6 UNMASKING MESSES

As they left the Finance Department, Alice was feeling a little bit taller. She felt like she had accomplished something and said the same to Penguin, "I feel like I accomplished something in the Finance Department."

"Of course you did. You showed up. You talked to them, and most importantly, you listened to them," answered Penguin, feeling quite proud of her.

"I wish I had learned everything I needed to know to clean up this mess. That way, I could go have a nice cup of tea and not have to think any more today." It was true Alice had made progress, but she still had a long way to go and this caused Penguin to sigh.

"Perhaps Puppy will tell us everything we need to know so we can understand how to clean it up," Penguin said encouragingly.

After walking a very long way, Alice and Penguin stepped through a door marked: Manufacturing. Upon entering, they stared, mouths hanging open. They saw Puppy bounding back and forth across the entire length of the large manufacturing building as fast as his legs would carry him. Alice and Penguin continued to stand as close to the wall as possible, hoping Puppy wouldn't see them. It had been a very long time since Alice had visited, and she'd forgotten how enormous he was. His head was almost as high as the ceiling, and he could travel the length of the building in just a few strides, where it would take Alice several minutes to walk from one end to the other.

As Alice and Penguin continued to watch, they soon discovered he was playing fetch. When something was needed, Puppy would scramble to retrieve it. They watched this process for several minutes, seeing how the workers had cleverly learned to avoid the dog's huge paws.

Alice, still unwilling to move away from the relative safety of the wall, called out to a worker who was crouched behind a pile of drums nearby. "Why don't you simply move what you need from the end where it isn't needed to the end where it is needed?" The frown lines on her forehead furrowed her brow.

"That is an excellent question," responded the worker. Alice saw him give a start and shrink back against the wall even further as the dog scampered past them so closely it generated a wind causing Alice's hair to blow into her eyes.

"And do you have an excellent answer?" inquired Alice smoothing her hair.

"How would *you* like to ask him a question?" and the worker jerked his head in the direction of the pup who couldn't control his momentum and skittered into a few barrels that were off to the side, knocking them over.

"I guess I wouldn't," she replied.

"We have tried, but he still doesn't listen. We have shown him the procedures manual, but he doesn't seem to care. All he wants to do is to chase and fetch." With that, the worker waved good-bye for this was his chance to run to the next area of cover while the puppy was at the other end.

"I don't understand how this has happened," exclaimed Alice. I need to talk with Puppy. She put her fists on her hips and bravely marched out to confront the oversized Manufacturing Manager. As he came tearing back, Alice shouted at the top of her voice, "Sit!" Puppy was surprised at this and immediately sat down, his tongue lolling out of his mouth as he panted. "Stay," added Alice. "I have a few questions to ask you. Please explain what is going on here," she said in a way she hoped sounded authoritative but not accusatory. She had learned in the finance department that if she wanted cooperation, she needed *not* to put people on the defensive.

Puppy was obviously glad the girl had come to talk to him and he lay down at her feet, but his head still towered above her. Alice craned her neck to look up at him and asked, "Why isn't the procedures manual being followed?

At just that moment, someone yelled, "We need a yellow jockeywoober at this end." With that, Puppy bolted up, turned around, and ran to the far end of the building. With Puppy gone, several other workers quickly approached Alice and gave her grand praise for so fearlessly facing the giant dog. "Brave, you must be!" exclaimed one awestruck worker.

"Nonsense," exclaimed Alice, "he's just a puppy. He's big, to be sure, but he means well."

"That he may," asserted the second worker, "but you never have to clean up his messes and we do."

"Messes?" asked Alice, remembering she had come here looking for answers about the mess she had learned of earlier. "What kind of messes?"

"All sorts of messy messes," the third worker told her.

"How do you clean up the messes?" Perhaps she would finally get the information she needed.

"Usually we have to get into a lot of hot water in order to clean up the mess," offered the second worker.

"Yes, but sometimes that doesn't work," added the first, "so we have to mask it with an excessive amount of red tape."

"Does that make it better?" Alice asked, hoping she finally had her solution.

"No, almost never," responded the first worker.

"Then why do you do it?" she asked feeling more and more confused.

"Well, all that red tape looks frightening so folks don't go near it," the third worker offered.

Feeling frustrated, Alice asked, "When does it ever get cleaned up?"

"Why never, of course!" answered the second worker and all three had a good laugh as they pointed around the building where Alice now noticed large areas masked with an excessive amount of red tape.

Penguin pulled on Alice's skirt to get her attention, and motioned for her to bend down in order to whisper in her ear. After listening to him, she straightened herself and said, "That is an excellent question, Penguin. I will ask them." Turning to the three workers, she inquired, "As your manager, isn't it Puppy's job to help you clean up messes rather than create them?"

"Of course it is, but he doesn't understand that yet. He's untrained. Sure, he's full of enthusiasm, but that doesn't do a lick of good unless he points his enthusiasm in the right direction," answered the first worker, and the others all nodded their heads in agreement.

"Well, why is he the supervisor and not someone who has been trained and understands what is expected of the manufacturing department?"

"I suppose you'd have to talk with HR about that," responded worker number three.

"HR?" asked Alice. "Do you mean HRH – Her Royal Highness?"

"'Course not." exclaimed the second worker. He then had a second thought. "Wait! Who *are* you?"

With that, Penguin cleared his throat and nodded toward the door indicating it was time for them to leave. Alice gave a small courtesy and graciously thanked the three workers for helping her. She promised she would come back someday soon.

Once outside, Alice asked Penguin, "why did we need to leave so suddenly?"

"I was afraid we were going to become one of Puppy's messes. It is tiring to constantly avoid his paws. In addition, it didn't seem like we were going to learn anything more. We already received the information we needed the most."

"But, who is this HR person who has put Puppy in a position for which he isn't trained?"

Penguin didn't show his surprise that Alice wasn't familiar with HR and their role at Leaves-of-Wonderland. Instead of questioning her, he simply guided her in the direction in which they needed to go in order to reach the HR office. "Alice, you didn't explain to them who you are when you asked questions."

"I didn't feel it was necessary. Besides, they answered all my questions."

"Yes, but it might have helped you to learn more. Also, they might have felt honored to meet you and have tried harder to work with Puppy just because you asked." He didn't want to add that her mysterious visit probably further contributed to the scent of unease in the already fetid air.

WORKBOOK
6 UNMASKING MESSES

SUMMARY

After leaving the finance department, Alice and Penguin continue their journey in pursuit of information. Their next stop is Manufacturing, which the pair have been led to believe by the finance department is where all the problems are generated.

Upon entering Manufacturing, Alice and Penguin witness Puppy, the enormous, overly exuberant department manager running to and fro, playing fetch and carry down the length of the building. As the workers try to stay hidden from him, Alice bravely steps up and demands his full attention. Unfortunately, before she has an opportunity to get answers from him regarding the other department's accusations, Puppy bounds off on an errand to deliver something needed at the other end of the building.

Three workers who had seen Alice confront the giant pooch came out of hiding to congratulate her on being so brave. They don't realize who she is, but they know she must be important to have Penguin as her escort. Thus, they were more than happy to answer her questions about Manufacturing. Alice quickly learns procedures are not followed because, in spite of his exuberance, Puppy has had no training and doesn't know how to channel his energy. This has caused many big messes, which the workers have to clean up. With a bit more questioning, Alice learns that, in fact they are never really cleaned up – they are merely masked with an excessive amount of red tape.

Hearing all of this, Alice is feeling a bit exasperated, wondering why Puppy was put in such a position of responsibility with no training, and the three workers explain to her HR is responsible. Alice assumes they must be referring to the Queen, HRH, but they assure her they mean HR. Penguin is able to lead her away from the employees before they discover she is Alice, the founder of the company, and she doesn't know what or who HR is.

WHAT ALICE LEARNS

- How to be assertive without being accusatory, argumentative or condescending.

- Others respect her, and appreciate it when she is willing to step up and take a risk because it shows her confidence.

- Unbridled energy and enthusiasm without training and direction towards achieving a goal, can be counter-productive.

What other lessons do you see Alice has encountered in this chapter?

_____
_____
_____
_____
_____
_____

DISCUSSION QUESTIONS

1. In this chapter we can see Alice is becoming a bit humbler. What evidence do you see of that happening?

2. How would you advise Alice to handle the Puppy situation?

3. In your opinion, what was the most important thing Alice learned during her visit to Manufacturing? Why?

SHORT ANWER QUESTIONS

1. Puppy is to blame for the messes in manufacturing.
   ___True   ___False

   Why do you feel this way?

2. The <u>biggest</u> mistake Alice made during this visit was:

   a. Not to have put a leash on Puppy when she had an opportunity

   b. Not introducing herself, assuming everyone would know her

   c. Not firing the employees who mask Puppy's messes

   d. Not knowing what HR stands for

   Why do you feel this is the biggest mistake?

3. In Chapter 5, the Finance team told Alice Manufacturing was responsible for the financial messes. Are the problems in Manufacturing the root cause of the issues in the other departments or are they symptoms of a greater problem?

   a. They are the root cause
   b. They are symptoms of a greater problem
   c. Don't know – it's too early to tell for sure

7 A ROYAL PAIN

Alice and Penguin walked away from the manufacturing area toward HR. It had been exhausting to watch Puppy bounding around. The whole department was chaotic.

Alice was angry about this HR character who had made such bad decisions, including putting Puppy in a management role, and putting her company in jeopardy. Alice became singularly fixated on finding the focal point of her wrath. She was eager to foist the blame for all that was wrong upon this one department. That would solve all her problems with a simple solution. "Yes, putting the blame on HR would solve everything quite nicely" she thought. Alice was looking for the panacea to Leaves-of-Wonderland's current bad fortune and the manufacturing department had supplied her with it. She simply had to fix that awful HR with the tools and staff at her disposal. After all, she was the all powerful founder as both Penguin and Caterpillar had reminded her. She could command change and it would be done.

Alice felt a growth spurt coming over her. She was growing again! Or, was it just her ego that was growing? That awareness knocked Alice for a loop and she almost stumbled on a tree branch. Luckily, Penguin grabbed her before she fell so she only lost her balance for but a second, and, therefore, did not lose her dignity in a clumsy head-over-heels splat.

The two seemed to be moving in the right direction now, venturing forward to HR. Yet while Alice was momentarily distracted by her stumble, Penguin clasped her hand firmly with his flipper and pulled her in another direction, away from the straight and narrow path they had been following. "Alice, this direction is the best direction. We need to gather additional information before we present our situation to HR, and that additional information is conveniently nearby."

"Where are you taking me, Penguin? I thought we had the same goal in mind: finding HR. Isn't that our main focus now?" Alice was caught by surprise with Penguin's change of direction. She was so angry there was practically steam coming out of her ears. The combination of seeing three departments in turmoil, her near accidental fall that would've surely made her lose all grace and dignity, and finally, her overwhelming thoughts of grandeur, only to be yanked away by a pintsized overly-dressed assistant was too much for one girl's head. She felt pulled in too many different directions and it sent her thoughts into a dizzying fashion.

"What more can we possibly need to hear and see? I've had quite enough already. We've already gathered enough evidence to prove HR is not doing a proper job."

Alice crossed her arms and she wore a cranky look on her face, as she continued to complain, "One department with problems I could have handled, Penguin, but three so far? Why, it's madness! And speaking of madness, where is Hatter? What is my President doing through all of this, I wonder?"

After all their time together, Penguin knew how to best handle his boss' difficult moments. He said calmly with quiet conviction, "The Duchess in the quality control department is nearby, Alice. It makes sense to see her first. After all, she is supposed to control what gets shipped out of manufacturing. Maybe she has some answers".

Alice realized she had tired of her sudden growth and longed to be smaller again, having someone else take control. The enormity of her headache made her feel humbled. She was tired and no longer in a position to argue. She wanted to take a back seat. Alice didn't want to lead anymore, so she relented and followed Penguin. "That sounds logical, Penguin" she muttered.

Penguin pulled his fearless leader along until they heard a sharp noise: a pig squeal. "Oh, this must be Duchess' area. She's trying to play Momma to that pig again! I've never understood her fascination with the pig. She tries to mother it like it's her baby and all it ever does is squeal. Why be associated with a pig?" The two were oblivious to the fact that all the other departments had their own squealing mechanism; they had all squealed on another department for their own mishandlings.

Alice and Penguin followed the sound of the squealing until they came into an area not too far away from Manufacturing. "Here we are, Alice" explained Penguin.

And there was Duchess and her staff including her right hand, the Chef, directly in their sight. Alice and Penguin came up from behind Duchess and surprised her.

Duchess had been barking reprimands at her staff when the two approached. "Chef, this tea has too much spice. How could you not catch this? It's lacking a pinch of sweetness that should be in a spiced tea. It has too much bite!"

Alice reached out to tap Duchess' shoulder when the woman, feeling their presence, quickly reeled around to face the intruders. "Who dares to interrupt me?" she thundered, only to quickly change her demeanor once she realized it was the founder of the company. Then she smiled with false reverence and said sweetly, "Oh, it's you. How nice to see you!" The ugly, mad face melted quickly into a huge grin.

"Why, Duchess, you look quite like Cheshire Cat right now" Alice exclaimed.

"What?" she sputtered feeling the threads of an insult. She quickly remembered herself and her position, and restarted her words with an ingratiating tone. "Why have you come to honor me with your esteemed presence? What can I possibly do to help you?" She then bowed as low as her enormous head would allow her.

Alice responded ignoring the unctuous tone of the Duchess, "I have come to look upon your operations. Penguin and I wanted to see how you are doing." She further explained, "You know, Puppy has Manufacturing in quite an uproar and we, or rather I, thought you might have control of the leash and know how to keep him in line."

"Oh, of course," Duchess smiled. "Yes, I can control the undisciplined pooch, but why should I? It's not my department. It's not my responsibility". She bragged with confidence at the same time dismissing the bumbling Puppy. She wiped her hands on her apron which was already smeared with brown tea stains as if to wipe away the lunacy of the thought she should be responsible for that mangy mutt.

"You can? Not after what we just saw: the fenced off messes, the constant motion. Puppy doesn't read so he can't follow the procedure manual, and his employees are afraid and so no one speaks to him. Consequently, there is no one to teach him the rules.

"What good is a procedure manual when one doesn't follow what it says? The company needs rules and procedures so it can operate like it is supposed to. Things must be organized in an organization in an organized fashion. " barked Penguin.

Alice held her finger to her lips and turned to face the little Penguin. She had found it was nice being led for a little while, but she could see she needed to quickly regain her stature because Penguin didn't seem to be making the right impression. "Shh, Penguin. Let me handle this." She turned back to face the older woman. "Duchess, if Puppy is undisciplined then there is no one to blame except you. He's just a puppy. He needs consistency in his training. That is surely the best thing for him. With his erratic behavior, I can only guess the commands he's been receiving are unsettling and therefore he is confused."

At that utterance the Duchess flinched and then again remembering herself, spoke in her sweetest voice. "Oh, but you haven't heard me speaking with him so how would you really know? Can it be you are making false accusations? What is your real knowledge of the situation? Perhaps you are being too hasty in your perceptions and you are jumping to a false conclusion?" She thought the best tactic would be to seemingly appease Alice into believing she had already tried to reason with Puppy to eliminate his bad behavior.

Alice heard the duchess and pondered what she had to say. Perhaps she did have a point: she'd never actually heard Duchess address Puppy. Alice had learned something in an earlier part of her journey through the departments, and she would not jump to conclusions and would give Duchess a chance to explain herself. "Well, perhaps I don't know the entire story, Duchess." But then her earlier sense of self-importance knowing she was the founder of Leaves-of-Wonderland came back to her and she blurted, "But it seems Puppy doesn't know any better, and if you are training him, then it is up to you to teach him properly!"

At that moment, Chef clattered the bottles he was examining, and they all looked up at him. Duchess shrieked, "Can't you keep quiet for even a few minutes while our leader is here? Can't you do your job right," and then she added sneakily, "like I've trained you to do?" And with that she smiled yet again at her own brilliant performance. Chef went back to his work, ignoring the sharp-tongued woman.

"I don't know, Duchess, but I've witnessed that you can be

quite nice and then you can easily slip into frustration at a little mishap and become short-tempered".

"She's quite right, you know. You are not a model of good behavior. You have no patience. And to be training a puppy with no patience is an accident waiting to happen," said Penguin, almost unaware of the fact he had spoken.

"Penguin, quiet!" Alice snapped. Her rudeness was a result of her own impatience with Duchess who was not prepared to accept responsibility for her behavior.

Duchess slipped her arm around the girl's shoulder. "Thank you for coming to my rescue," she said in a coy tone as she led Alice out of the department and onto the garden path. Penguin waddled quickly to catch up to them. "I'm sure you'll find there is someone else to blame for Puppy's behavior. You know, the quality of Leaves-of-Wonderland teas has never been in question. Our company has always been praised for that, so why don't you just worry your pretty, little head about something else, now, hmmm?" And with that Alice found herself dismissed by her own employee.

WORKBOOK
7 A ROYAL PAIN

SUMMARY

Alice and Penguin have barely made it out of the manufacturing area with their lives intact. They are as breathless as the manufacturing workers who suffer under the boundless unpredictable direction of Puppy. The mismanagement of this key department causes Alice's anger and mistrust of HR, which would hire such a disaster and leave him to his own devices, to increase exponentially. This misplaced anger leads her to the cowardly decision of blaming all the woes she has encountered thus far on HR as the one and only culprit. In putting all the blame on HR, Alice feels she has miraculously saved her company and feels very full of her own superiority.

Amidst her positive self-affirmation, however, Penguin has other ideas: he attempts to steer his boss away from their road to HR and bring her back to her senses with a touch of reality and tough love. He leads her to visit Duchess in Quality Control to view how her department is functioning. Alice and Penguin are unwelcome guests, annoying Duchess with their badgering - questioning the department head's behavior and her responsibilities.

Duchess is not pleased by a surprise visit whose primary intention is to embarrass her about something she feels clearly is not in her job description nor of primary concern. Duchess, in her own inimitable fashion, tries to stifle her condescension of Alice while protecting herself from the duo's accusations, but isn't quite as convincing as she might have hoped (although does she really care?). The cunning department head evades blame, takes control of the situation, and is able to dismiss the founder of the company and her assistant quite easily so she can return to her ever important work.

WHAT ALICE LEARNS

- Loyalty is underrated.

- Strong emotions such as anger can cloud effective decision-making, which can lead to grave mistakes. Sometimes you need to take a break from an escalating situation, do something else and then return to it with new perspective and a clearer mind.

- Anyone can be vulnerable in a meeting, no matter their role or title, if they aren't prepared.

    What other lessons do you see Alice has encountered in this chapter?

    _____
    _____
    _____
    _____
    _____
    _____

DISCUSSION QUESTIONS

1. Was Alice well prepared for her meeting with Duchess? If you had been Alice how would you have prepared differently? Why?

2. How would you describe the feelings Duchess has toward Alice? How does she feel about her job? Are the two connected?

3. From the way Duchess seems to run her department, would she make a better leader than Alice? If so, why? What do you like or dislike about her style of leadership?

SHORT ANSWER QUESTIONS

1. Do you feel Duchess is an asset to the company or a liability?

   Why?

2. Penguin is helpful to Alice in this chapter.

   True___   False___

3. What does the squealing pig symbolize in the chapter and/or in the story so far?

   a. A dissatisfied employee
   b. A dissatisfied customer
   c. Alice
   d. The Duchess
   e. The cat-fight between the two females
   f. The shrill voice of some of the complainers and blamers in the story
   g. Don't care

   Why did you select this answer?

8 TEA TOTALING

Alice and Penguin looked at each other confounded by their predicament: they were placed on the garden path by a bossy Duchess and not by their own conscious efforts. "That woman! How dare she? She deposited us outside Quality Control like a rejected tea bag, like trash!" Alice hated to admit it but Penguin had a point.

"Penguin, I'm tired. Can we please find someplace to sit while I ponder all that has happened so far today? Duchess' bad behavior is just the tip of the iceberg." Penguin could relate to Alice's admission and he was tired too. He searched the nearby vicinity for a place the two could sit, but was unable to find a suitable spot.

"I don't see anything, but perhaps if we start walking in the direction of HR, we will find a nice soft bed of grass. At least, we will be headed in the right direction." The two walked on, hand in flipper to give each other physical support.

It did not take too long, thankfully. Penguin soon spotted a nice open area of soft grass-cover sprinkled with pretty purple wild flowers and two nice-sized toadstools. "There, Alice!" and he pointed toward the haven ahead of them.

"That looks heavenly, Penguin!" She was barely able to get out a loud whisper, she was so exhausted. Alice sought out the comfort of the slightly bigger toadstool while Penguin flopped down on the grass.

"If you don't mind, Alice, I don't feel like climbing right now. My legs are tired."

It didn't really matter to her where he sat as long as she could talk with him. "Suit yourself" she said carelessly.

Penguin reached into his back pocket and pulled out a

Thermos of Leaves-of-Wonderland iced tea he had brewed earlier. Thwack! He took the two cups off the top of the Thermos and poured the beverage for Alice first, and then for himself. Alice heard the opening of the vacuum of the Thermos and turned around. She saw how Penguin had made the grass so inviting and her mouth watered at the thought of something to drink. Alice smiled at his resourcefulness and his manners. "I'll join you on the grass," and she flopped next to him.

Alice and Penguin drank their cold tea without a word at first. The two had been so thirsty for knowledge and answers they had forgotten how thirsty their bodies were, so they drank quickly and with gusto. When the cups were emptied, Penguin refilled them. "Yum! This is sooo good! This is a new flavor, isn't it, Penguin?"

Penguin puffed up his tightly feathered torso, proclaiming proudly, "I made it myself. I brewed a few of our teabags together to make this. Isn't it nice?"

"Hmm... What is it and what do you call it?"

"I haven't got a name for it...Perhaps we should call it, "Penguin's Protection" laughed Penguin reflecting on their long day and what was yet to come.

"It has a little bit of Echinacea, vitamin C, and a number of different detoxifying ingredients. I can't remember them all. When I mixed it this morning, I had a suspicion I could use some extra vitamins to fortify me in case any burdens came our way. Always better to be safe..."

"I like it!" said Alice and she laughed too. Penguin had so many talents. She would have to remember that and reward him for it. Perhaps he could even make suggestions to, or work part-time in, research and development. He would probably like that. She made a mental note to herself.

"That was good thinking, Penguin. But how could you know what the day would be like?"

"I had a feeling this morning it was going to be a busy day. But I didn't know it was going to be quite like this".

Alice and Penguin rested and then Alice resumed talking. Rest and the beverage had a way of clearing Alice's head and she began to be ashamed of her earlier behavior with her companion.

"Penguin" she started, "you will have to excuse me. I am afraid I did you an awful disservice. I have been taking my frustration out on you. I've been doing nothing but criticizing you all day. You deserve my gratitude, not my scolding. You have been a most constant ally and friend. You have stood by me and I should be standing by you proudly...."

Penguin stopped listening. She was embarrassing him. In his mind, he had just been doing his job as any loyal assistant would do - nothing special. He had been reflecting on the faith she had shown in him when he awoke from his reveries to her continuing....

".....I ssshed you in front of Duchess."

"Enough, enough! You hired me when I was not up to the task. You saw my potential when no one else did. Hatter didn't. The Queen of Hearts and the Board didn't. Because you did, I will be forever grateful. I hold my head up high because of you! I know you are not perfect, no one is... I know you have short comings: I know you become frustrated sometimes which causes you to get angry, or teary, or short-tempered like," he paused trying to recall who she resembled when she became irritable and short-tempered. Then, the comparison became clear. ".. like Duchess, but I know YOU mean nothing by your outbursts." He took a breath to emphasize his sentiments.

"You are growing, Alice. I am prouder to be working alongside you, than ever before, because you are taking responsibility for your actions and standing up to bullies and listening to others...." As he chattered on about how proud he was of her, his head was held higher.

"Well, then, Penguin, I guess we have done it together! For we both have grown." It was impossible to miss his admirable attempts at making himself taller. It almost made her want to cry in response to the devotion he had expressed for her. Not wanting to upset him further with her tears, and knowing they did not need a pond, which might result from her crying too much, she focused intently on her words instead. "You grew into your role as my hardworking assistant and I am beginning to become a better leader. We have become stronger individually by working as a team than if we did not have each other to learn from. I am better at my job because of your support." She gave him a moment to hear her words and understand she was complimenting him. "What do you say now to that?" she smiled.

Penguin liked that the extreme attention was taken off him and put on both of their shoulders to share. That was much more comfortable and realistic for him. Penguin flapped his flippers together furiously in a loud clapping sound. He liked hearing his support was helping her. Alice felt good making Penguin happy and also felt good acknowledging and complimenting someone who deserved it. She liked the way complimenting felt!

"Unlike Duchess, you know how to compliment with sincerity." said Penguin and he winked. "She should have shown you more respect, Alice. She should not have pushed us out of Quality Control, even if she did it with her arm around your shoulders. That was very sly of her; she gave you the cold shoulder, when it should have been YOU who was delivering any of that treatment!"

Alice acknowledged Penguin was bringing up the subject of Duchess' behavior yet again, but added "It wasn't as bad as you make it out to be. She wanted to get back to her work, Penguin. She had a lot of tea to examine and not much time to get it all done. Duchess has a very busy department and schedule. We interrupted her rhythm. She simply wanted to tell me what I needed to know and then get back to business. I can understand that."

"Oh, but Missy, you can't have been unaware of the way she MIStreated you." (Penguin was trying to make a comment he didn't want Alice to miss. He waved his flipper with emphasis). "You must acknowledge she could have handled herself like the titled lady that she is, with dignity, and then given you the dignity and respect you deserve. You hired her, not the other way around. She answers to you. Alice, you still must learn to stand up to your critics and your subordinates when they need to be put in their place. You deserve respect."

Alice agreed Penguin was right again, but only to a certain degree. She didn't judge Duchess as harshly as he did. "Now, now, Duchess performs her job in Quality Control well. She has some good qualities: we need her expertise and she has saved us from a lot of mishaps. She runs her own department very strictly, with much regard for Wonderland pride and procedure, even if she doesn't put quite that amount of effort into overseeing Manufacturing and Puppy. Perhaps because it really is another department and NOT her DIRECT responsibility. We have not allowed much spoiled tea to make it out of our doors since she's been in charge of Quality Control". Alice made another mental note to bring in a trainer to either train Duchess or Puppy directly.

Penguin made himself laugh - "That's because she puts all the spoiledness into the piglet she coddles like her baby. She won't let him out of her sight."

Alice tried to stop herself from laughing, but the vision of Duchess struggling with the pig in her arms got the better of her, and she laughed too. Penguin and Alice needed the laugh after their stressful day. "It's not nice to laugh at another's expense….. but, we needed that. Now we have that out of our system, we can return to our day without delay. So, let's share our findings from today's experiences and then we can pursue the path of HR. We haven't solved our puzzle, but we have some major pieces to insert". Penguin inched closer to Alice so as not to miss any details or lessons Alice might impart to him about Operations, Finance, Manufacturing, or Quality Control.

They were laying out the pieces of their puzzle when a loud rustling of leaves caused them to look up and around. Alice and Penguin didn't see anything at first and it became very quiet again. They became confident it was nothing and were just about to resume their briefing when they heard the noise again. They both gulped when they saw Hatter, the brim of his hat covering his eyes. His large shaded head had emerged from behind a big oak tree into their view. He had taken a misstep from behind the tree and had lost his footing which had caused the hat to fall over his face. Or, had he been hiding behind both the trunk and his hat to begin with? Regardless, apparently, he had been hiding there for some time. He had heard their conversation, although, it wasn't clear how much.

"Oh, excuse me. I must have taken a wrong turn in my haste to meet the Board for tea. It was such an immediate invitation, you see. I had no time to prepare. I must answer to them you know, but for what, I don't know. Why, yes, but you know how impatient that woman can be and you know how happy she is to cut off someone's head. I don't want to be that person. Would you? I'll be off then. Good-bye." As quickly as he appeared, he disappeared, running down an alternative muddy track, a fork in the garden path Alice and Penguin had been following.

His appearance chilled them or perhaps it was a combination of the rustling leaves he had caused in his wake and the temperature of the iced tea they had just finished. Nevertheless, his countenance had bewildered them. What would Hatter be doing, hiding behind a tree, listening to them, unless he was up to something? It was an ill wind that blew in his wake.

WORKBOOK
8 TEA TOTALING

SUMMARY

After being summarily dismissed from Quality Control by Duchess, Alice and Penguin need a respite before continuing their odyssey. After all, this was yet another bit of evidence Leaves-of-Wonderland is in turmoil, and thus, increased the stress Alice was feeling. Neither of them is in any condition to continue on down the path to confront HR. So, their first order of business is to find a place to stop and catch their breath.

As the two settle in a nice shady spot, Penguin produces a thermos of tea – a healing elixir of his own concoction – Penguin's Protection. After a few sips, the pair are feeling much better, and Alice, once again, marvels at the many talents her loyal assistant possesses. This causes her to reflect on how she has mistreated him during their journey, especially during their visit with Duchess.

It's difficult for Penguin to receive credit or to accept Alice's apologies. Thus, he quickly reminds her she was the one who took the risk to hire him when no one else saw his potential. Therefore, all the credit is hers.

As their conversation continues, they disagree about Duchess: Alice considers her to be an asset to the company, while Penguin finds her to be disrespectful of Alice, and thus, he has little to say on her behalf.

Suddenly, their conversation is interrupted by a rustling of leaves. There hiding behind a tree is Hatter. He quickly offers excuses as to why he is there, but the two mistrust his intentions. They feel he has been spying on them, listening to every word they said. But why? With no further explanation, Hatter begs their pardon and is off to meet with the Queen of Hearts and the rest of the Board of Directors, leaving Alice and Penguin feeling increasingly uncertain.

WHAT ALICE LEARNED

- There can be more depth to a person than their job description or job duties might indicate.

- They need to take time out of the bustle of their work environment to gather and analyze their findings in order for them to have a renewal of purpose.

- Alice has an ability to see the worth of an individual when others may not be as aware.

    What other lessons do you see Alice has encountered in this chapter?

    _____
    _____
    _____
    _____
    _____

DISCUSSION QUESTIONS:

1. A good leader can often see positive attributes in people others may not see, and Alice is beginning to have this ability. Therefore, no one is one hundred percent good or bad. She is able to get a more realistic assessment of those who work for her, and perhaps of herself as well. If you were the CEO, would you fire Duchess for her behavior (as Penguin would have suggested) or would you have adopted Alice's point of view and valued her positive qualities above her negative qualities?

   Why would you take this position?

2. How would you advise Alice to handle her concerns regarding the incident with Hatter?

3. Does Penguin deflect Alice's apologies so she feels better about herself? If so, what do you feel is his motivation?

SHORT ANSWER QUESTIONS

1. Alice and Penguin's break for tea was an important part of their day. Do you agree?

   ___ Yes   ___ No

   Why or why not?

2. Alice was insulted by Duchess' treatment of her.

   ___ True   ___ False

   What evidence is there to support your answer?

3. The Duchess will best be able to assist Alice by…? (write your best response)

9 BIRD BRAINS

Hatter's unsettling appearance had been a reminder to Alice and Penguin they had little time to complete their journey to uncover the truth and regain control of Leaves-of-Wonderland. Thus, they were back on the path of discovery once again.

They walked quickly in stunned silence, neither wanting to bring up the confrontation that had just happened. Finally, Penguin could be quiet no longer. "Hatter's appearance chilled me to the bone. It felt odd and uncomfortable and I don't know what to make of it. I am not sure what we can do about it?"

"What's there to remedy? What is the problem? Hatter was being sneaky, but to what end? Do we know? And if we don't know, what can we try to change? Do you see my point?" questioned Alice. "Why don't we try to solve what we are more able to solve and continue our original plan toward reaching HR."

As they made their way toward the HR department, Penguin trying to put Hatter out of his mind, changed the subject and asked, "Alice, have you ever met your legal department?"

"No, I have not." responded Alice. "Should I have?"

"Of course! The legal department influences many decisions within the company. If they are not doing their job correctly, it will not be good for you or Leaves-of-Wonderland," explained the assistant in a most insightful manner.

"Then I shall meet them someday soon. I don't want to have to worry about people making bad decisions," Alice exclaimed decisively.

"Well, may I suggest we stop and meet them now as we will be passing The Nest on our way to HR?"

"Certainly, you may suggest it, Penguin," Alice told him. When he didn't respond, she added, "Well, aren't you going to suggest it?"

"Yes, of course," and the little chap cleared his throat and said, "Alice, I suggest we stop by The Nest and meet the Legal Department."

"That is an excellent suggestion, Penguin. But, what is The Nest?"

"It is where all the Legal Eagles congregate."

"Really? That's wonderful. I am so happy we employ Legal Eagles. I agree with you. They are very important to the company" she responded with mounting excitement over the prospect of meeting them.

"Well," Penguin interjected, "we don't really."

"We don't what?" asked Alice.

"We don't employ Legal Eagles."

"Oh, but you just said…"

"I said," clarified Penguin, "The Nest is where all the Legal Eagles gather, but none of them work for Leaves-of-Wonderland."

"Oh, I see," she murmured when, in fact, she didn't see at all. "Penguin, you are talking in circles. Tell me what you mean."

He realized Alice was confused, and since Penguin had taken it upon himself to help her become enlightened, he certainly didn't want to be the cause of more confusion. Therefore, he offered an explanation, which he hoped would clarify matters for her. "The Legal Eagles only reside at The Nest before and after work. There are other lawyers who may not be.. well, they aren't exactly lawyers. They are 'almost-lawyers'. And those almost-lawyers work for you."

Seeing Alice was still confused, Penguin thought about providing further explanation, but decided she would soon learn all she needed to learn from the Legal Department. "Alice, it will be easier for you to understand what I'm trying to say once you see The Nest for yourself."

When the pair arrived at The Nest, they stepped inside to see the only two individuals there besides themselves were the Mock Turtle and Gryphon, otherwise known as the Legal Department of Leaves-of-Wonderland. Having never seen Alice, neither Mock Turtle nor Gryphon recognized her. Consequently, they didn't know their employer stood before them or they might have reacted differently.

"Are you an Attorney at Law?" demanded Gryphon in his very

best cross-examination voice?

"Why no, but..." began Alice.

However, she was cut off mid-sentence by Mock Turtle who continued to grill the witness, "Then what are you doing here?"

"Don't you know what The Nest is?" asked Gryphon pointing his talon in Alice's face. She opened her mouth to answer, and what her answer would have been we'll never know because before she had a chance to say a word Gryphon interrupted by answering his own question. "Of course you don't know what The Nest is because you are not an Attorney at Law."

With this, Mock Turtle took up the argument saying, "The Nest is only for Attorneys at Law. You do not belong here."

"That is correct, Counselor," exclaimed Gryphon, slapping Mock Turtle on the back. "We belong here because we are Attorneys at Law and we have diplomas to prove it."

"I see," Alice was finally able to interject. "What I don't see is why you are here and not working."

"We are here because The Nest is the bar every Attorney at Law must pass on the way to work. My fellow Attorney here and I just never seem to be able to pass it. So, this is where we spend our days. Everyone knows it, and if they need us to resolve some pressing legal issue, they bring the matter to us here," explained Mock Turtle while the Gryphon stood at his side nodding his head in agreement.

"Now, young lady, we suggest you leave this establishment," stated Gryphon in a manner that indicated it really wasn't a suggestion as much as a directive.

"I will when I'm good and ready, and I'm neither good nor ready," responded Alice causing the two to take a step back. They were quite unused to anyone questioning them since interrogation was their responsibility, and the right with which they had been endowed by virtue of their impressive diplomas. As they stood before her uncharacteristically speechless, Alice asked them, "Do you know who I am?"

Regaining some of their composure, the two took turns throwing out a barrage of questions in response to Alice: "Who do *you* think you are?", "Why should we care who you are if you don't know yourself?", "What business is it of yours who we think you are?", "When was the last time you knew who you were?", "Do you have a subpoena requiring us to answer that question?", and finally, "Has anyone suggested we should know who you are?"

"Stop!" yelled Alice at the top of her voice. It was the only way to get them to stop and listen to her. "Are you in the habit of answering a question with a question?" she demanded, but it was rhetorical and she didn't expect an answer.

However, it was a question, and neither Mock Turtle nor Gryphon could ignore such an opportunity, so they responded in unison, "What do you mean?"

"Exactly!" she exclaimed. "Now, look here, you two, I am Alice, the founder of Leaves-of-Wonderland! My company pays you to be at work helping to solve problems, not wasting your time here at the bar. How do you explain your actions?"

Mock Turtle and Gryphon were dumbfounded for a moment and simply stood and looked at one another and back at Alice. Finally, Gryphon found his voice and responded by asking, "In what context shall we explain our actions?"

Evidently Mock Turtle admired Gryphon's approach as he gave him a professional nod, and added his own response, "Furthermore, heretofore there has been no precedence requiring the party of the first part to respond to the party of the second part. If said requirements are now legislated, we must appeal to the court to provide us with ample opportunity to examine the evidence and amend our case. We are professionals. Thus, we shan't require an excessive length of time to prepare. Can we all agree to recess until, say two o'clock on the third Tuesday week after next?"

With this, Alice sadly realized yet another of her departments was lacking direction, professionalism and ability. With no further conversation, she turned and left The Nest. Penguin followed silently behind her.

Back on the path that would eventually take them to the HR department, Alice was unusually quiet as she pondered what had just occurred. Something was poking at her brain, trying to get her attention, but she couldn't quite figure out what it was. Then ever so slowly, the haze began to lift and Alice was able to see more clearly than she ever had before. Unfortunately, she didn't like all she saw.

Seeing the unhappy look on her face, Penguin asked Alice, "What is bothering you? You look as though you feel unwell."

Alice did look a bit unwell, at that. "I'm afraid," she said.

"Afraid? Of what are you afraid?" asked Penguin the concern

clearly evident in his voice.

"I'm afraid I don't like what I see." Now with her newly improved vision, she could clearly see Penguin didn't understand her, so she explained. "Look, we just left yet another department that is in total turmoil being run ineptly. A legal department? We call those two crazies the legal department? They can't even pass the bar let alone actually provide valuable advice. The worst part is I see I am a big part of the problem in the company, and I don't like that. I don't quite understand what I'm doing wrong, so I surely cannot do things correctly." After her tirade, Alice felt emotionally spent. "It isn't easy peering into the looking glass, and admitting you don't like what you see when what you see is you."

They continued down the path to a place where it forked. Alice hesitated for a moment and then sighed, "I'm so tired, I really don't want to have to go down another new path. Yet, I believe I should so I can see what it holds for me."

With that conviction they started down the new path. Penguin had been quiet for a very long time and Alice was wondering what was going through his mind. When she inquired, Penguin responded, "I was impressed by how you stood up to Gryphon and Mock Turtle. It hasn't been but a short time ago you would not have questioned them."

"Was that wrong of me?" asked Alice feeling a bit discomfited.

"Indeed no!" exclaimed Penguin. I was so proud of you."

Alice breathed a sigh of relief. She truly did want to please her assistant. "I don't want to be mean, but on the other hand, I feel it is my obligation to get the information necessary for my company to operate the best it can."

This change in attitude was quite a surprise, and Penguin was proud of her. This was a very important lesson for Alice. If she understood being assertive was perfectly within her right and was in no way being mean, then there was great hope for her. Penguin placed his flipper in the girl's hand and they continued on their way in search of more questions and, hopefully, some answers.

WORKBOOK
9 BIRD BRAINS

SUMMARY

Following their encounter with Hatter, the dynamic duo is filled with a sense of foreboding. They know time is of the essence, so they are once again on the path headed toward the increasingly infamous HR department.

Feeling a battle between Alice and her adversaries may be imminent; Penguin is compelled to take her to meet the legal team. Therefore, he proposes a detour to 'The Nest,' the bar all attorneys at law must pass before they can go to work.

Alice learns that, unfortunately, her legal team is not quite the kettle of 'legal eagles' she had hoped, but rather Griffin and Mock Turtle, two would-be attorneys who never quite seem to be able to pass the bar.

As has happened on some of her earlier stops, Alice isn't recognized by the two lone patrons of The Nest, and they severely challenge her right to enter the bar. However, Alice stands her ground, explaining she is the founder of Leaves-of-Wonderland. She demands an explanation as to why they are wasting their time at the bar when they are being paid to do legal work for the company.

Her frustrating, and somewhat baffling conversation with Griffin and Mock Turtle leaves Alice once again feeling low as she and Penguin resume their trek. At Penguin's questioning, Alice explains she is afraid she is largely responsible for all the things going wrong at the company. She confides that she doesn't even understand what it is she is doing wrong, so she surely doesn't know how to fix it.

As they continued their walk, Penguin is uncharacteristically quiet. When Alice asks him what's on his mind, he responds that he had been impressed by how she stood up to the two would-be lawyers. She still lacks confidence, and asks if it was appropriate for her to have acted as she did. Penguin assures her she handled the situation well. With a sigh of relief, she explains her behavior: She needs to gather as much information as is available to help her to make Leaves-of-Wonderland a success story.

WHAT ALICE LEARNED

- She is truly becoming a leader as she realizes she may not always be the direct cause of the issues at the company, but that does not alleviate her of the responsibility.

- Having courage doesn't mean you aren't afraid.

- Even when a leader acts a certain way, it doesn't mean they are 100% confident with their actions and decisions.

What other lessons do you see Alice has encountered in this chapter?

_____
_____
_____
_____
_____
_____

DISCUSSION QUESTIONS:

1. What is the pivotal moment for Alice in this chapter? Why?

2. Both Griffin and Mock Turtle look good on paper, but they have clearly been put in a position for which they are not prepared since they are unable to pass the bar. What are Alice's options to resolve this situation? Which of the options would you recommend and why?

3. Alice says that she doesn't know what she is doing wrong, so how can she do it correctly. If you were Alice's coach what are the primary points you would recommend that she work on? What suggestions would you give her about how to make progress?

SHORT ANSWER QUESTIONS:

1. Having two lawyers on staff who are unable to pass the bar is a bad business decision. Who do you assume is responsible?

    a. Alice

    b. HR

    c. Hatter

    d. Penguin

    e. Queen of Hearts

    f. Who knows?

2. Was Alice right in admitting to Penguin she didn't know if she acted correctly with the legal team?

    ___ Yes ___ No

    Why did you select this answer?

3. Did Alice gain enough information by visiting the legal team to make the detour worthwhile? _____Yes _____No

10 BEAVERLY ADVICE REVISITED

Alice and Penguin were both quiet as they traversed the path that would eventually carry them to HR. What was on each of their minds, we can only speculate.

For his part, Penguin was as difficult to pin down as Cheshire Cat, his expressions appeared then quickly disappeared only to be replaced by a new one. First, he wore a small smile that suggested all was right in the world. One can only assume this was a reflection of how pleased he was with the way the morning had gone. Alice had done quite well, and he noticed her hand had become more difficult to reach she had grown so much. Quickly, the look of contentment was replaced by a deep furrowed brow. Could this be a result of his worry that their next stop, the dreaded HR, would be more than Alice could handle? While Penguin, a fine chap indeed, was the picture of humility itself and never took credit for Alice's victories, he felt responsible when she didn't succeed. It was such a heavy burden for Penguin, and he gave a deep sigh as he pondered his responsibility.

Had she been listening, Alice would have heard Penguin's sigh and could have, perhaps, alleviated some of his concerns. As it was, she was deep in thought and was unaware of anything else. Judging by the stormy face worn by Alice, it is more than likely she was rehearsing the scene she would shortly have with HR. During her meetings, HR had become her sworn nemesis, in spite of the fact she knew little of the department's responsibilities. All that mattered was that things were a mess everywhere they went. Someone was to blame, and by all accounts, HR was the culprit.

"Therefore, you must fix the mess immediately," Alice blurted out. Hearing her own voice, Alice was so surprised she came to a sudden stop.

Penguin, equally surprised, looked at her quizzically and asked, "Of course, I am happy to help any way I can."

"Oh, no Penguin, I wasn't speaking to you. I was just thinking so loudly, I'm afraid my words tumbled out," replied Alice.

"You certainly sound different than you did earlier today," a third voice said. Alice and Penguin looked around to see who was listening to their conversation. As Alice spotted Beaver, still industriously at work on his dam, she couldn't help but smile. Earlier, perhaps she would have challenged that comment. Now, however, she was more confident and eager to share what she had learned. She was certain he would praise her for the wonderful things she had accomplished since they last spoke.

"Thank you, Beaver. I'm glad to see you, and delighted you noticed I have changed," she responded. Beaver paused in his work so he could give Alice a good looking-over. "Yes," he said, "there is something different about you. Why, I believe you have grown. Can that be true?"

"Yes!" exclaimed a very proud Alice. "I have grown so much today." Then a dark cloud passed over her countenance and she added more somberly, "But I'm afraid I have so much further to go."

"Don't frown, young lady - for you are carrying yourself like a young lady now, not merely a child. Don't frown, for growing is something that you never stop doing," said Beaver, confusing Alice. As she cocked her head to one side, trying to understand his meaning, Beaver offered a clarification by saying, "It is a journey, not a destination. Just as my teeth never stop growing, neither do we if we are wise, for there are always new opportunities to learn."

Alice's face brightened as she grasped his meaning. "That makes me feel much better. I like the idea of continuing to grow. I was afraid I had to do it all today and I couldn't figure out how."

Beaver picked up a branch in his paws to move to his construction site. "It's like this dam, Alice. I will finish this and it will give me great satisfaction to know I have accomplished this task. However, there is still much work remaining to control the stream. If and when I finish my work here, there are other waterways to redirect, other habitats for me to create. Now tell me, Alice, what have you done today that has helped you grow?"

Alice recounted her tale of visiting the various departments, and Penguin helped fill in the details which she had forgotten. To give Alice her due, she was quite objective, in her telling. She even shared with Beaver how she had fallen short. Beaver continued his task, stopping to look at her and ask questions from time to time. When Alice and Penguin were finished with their tale, they were both tired and found a nice toadstool upon which to settle.

No one spoke for a few minutes. Alice was holding her breath. For some reason, which she could not fathom, she wanted Beaver's approval. Penguin too held his breath for he also wanted Beaver's approval for Alice.

By and by, Beaver spoke, "You have had quite a day, young miss. How do you feel about what you have accomplished thus far?"

Alice was a tad disappointed he had not praised her and she pouted a bit before responding. "Why don't you tell me how you think I did?"

"Because," answered Beaver, giving her his full attention, "it really isn't important what I think. It is important what you think. If I give you praise, it is of little value if you don't believe it in your heart. If I offer you pointers, they are of little value unless you believe you have need for improvement."

Alice gave Beaver's comments great consideration. At first, she didn't like what he had said. She was like a child who wanted a treat for having been very, very good. After a bit, however, she soon understood, and appreciated that he was giving her a gift. Suddenly she sat up straight and exclaimed, "I understand. I have learned a lot, but there is so very much more for me to learn. Also, I'm afraid I will have to put all I have learned into practice. That will be most difficult, and I'm not at all sure how I will do it."

"That is very good, Alice. I can only assist you if you know you have need of assistance. Now, tell me: what is your next step?"

With this question, Alice seemed to puff up just a bit and she boldly said, "I am on my way to HR. They are the ones who have caused this horrible mess we are in and they must begin to clean it up at once."

"I see, and what is it HR does?"

Alice was caught a little off-guard with this question, "I'm not terribly sure. I know they are in charge of things."

"Aren't you also in charge of things?" queried Beaver.

"Well, yes, but they are in charge of people," Alice offered, sounding uncertain.

"And are you not also in charge of people?" Beaver asked, making Alice look deeper and deeper inside herself.

"Well, yes, I suppose so. Surely they are the ones who should be responsible."

"Responsible for what?"

"For…for….," Alice didn't have an answer for that. So, she put her chin back on her fist and sat on her toadstool while Beaver quietly went about his work, and Penguin sat and watched her. Finally, Alice lifted her head and exclaimed, "I don't know what they should be responsible for, I just know they should be."

"At least that is a beginning," Beaver replied.

"Well where shall I go from this beginning?"

"Alice, you already have the answer to that. More specifically, you already have the question for that," he replied, a faint smile playing at his lips. "Come back and tell me how it goes. I want to hear all about it." Beaver returned to his work and Alice and Penguin resumed their walk down the path to HR.

WORKBOOK
10 BEAVERLY ADVICE REVISITED

SUMMARY

Alice and Penguin continue on their travels toward HR, each one undergoing a multitude of emotions as they walk. Penguin's expressions change from moment to moment giving us a glimpse into his thoughts: his deepening respect for Alice and the progress they had made during their visits, and his worries about what lies ahead for them. Alice is so caught up in her own whirl of thoughts about her inevitable encounter with HR that words tumble out of her mouth that she had never intended to speak aloud. "What am I to do?".

Swept up by their emotions, they hadn't realized they were yet again in Beaver's territory, and the busy Beaver can't help but overhear their conversation. Noticing Alice's marked change, he compliments her, reminding her of the continual growth yet to come. Alice and Penguin tell Beaver all that has happened since they last met. Alice feels proud of her progress but she awaits further acknowledgement and direction from Beaver, which he refuses to give her unless she properly asks for it.

After she admits her lack of further direction and her need for help, Beaver speaks with them about Alice's next step: to visit HR. Alice unwittingly admits she is unsure of HR's role and responsibility. Beaver questions her about her intended approach to the "ominous" department in an effort to clarify Alice's beliefs and intentions. While he forces her to carefully consider her next plans, he is unwilling to tell her what she should do, he can only encourage her to formulate the best questions to ask HR so she will get the answers she needs to move forward in her goal. Beaver returns to his work. Alice and Penguin return to their path.

WHAT ALICE LEARNED

- Growth is a journey not a destination.

- Knowing what questions to ask is essential for acquiring the information you need to solve problems.

- Self-motivation and sense of self comes from within. They are necessary for growth. If you are always seeking confirmation and acknowledgment from others, you become dependent upon them and miss the opportunity to trust yourself to make decisions.

What other lessons do you see that Alice has encountered in this chapter?

_____
_____
_____
_____
_____
_____

DISCUSSION QUESTIONS:

1. What is Beaver's role in this chapter? Why do you feel he is an important figure to Alice?

    Do you agree with the advice that Beaver gave Alice? Do you agree with how he conveyed the advice to her?

2. What questions would you formulate for HR in preparation for the upcoming meeting?

3. Why is this chapter important to the story?

SHORT ANSWER QUESTIONS:

1. Which department meeting has been the most influential in Alice's growth up to this point?

    a. Operations

    b. Finance

    c. Manufacturing

    d. Quality control

    e. Legal

    Why did you select this answer?

2. Is Penguin jealous of Beaver's influence over Alice?

   ___ Yes   ___No

   Why did you select this answer?

3. What is causing the most dread for Alice in anticipation of the trip to HR?

11 A SMOKEY OMEN

As they rounded a corner on the path, Alice suddenly saw smoke climbing up into the sky. She became alarmed. Was there a fire? Did something go up in smoke? "Penguin, do you see that?" she asked her companion.

"What?"

"Those rings. Those rings of smoke. Where are they coming from?" She pointed.

Penguin raised his head. "Wow!" He was enthralled with the seemingly endless trail of O's. "Maybe it's an omen."

The possibilities for the cause of the smoke paraded through Alice's mind. She pulled Penguin forward. "Come, we must go and investigate. Someone may need help! Something at the company may be burning! This sidetrack is more important than resuming our path."

The two quickened their pace and followed the root of the rings until they arrived at their origination. What they saw made Alice breathe a sigh of relief. It was just Caterpillar, his glasses falling down his face as he puffed in contemplation, sitting on the biggest toadstool in the area. "It's you, Caterpillar!" cried Penguin.

"Of course, it's me. You are in my toadstool haven. Who else could it be?"

"Caterpillar, you scared us. We saw your signals from far away and thought you needed help." explained Alice.

"Really? Why would I need help?" He took a minute and then shook his head. "I don't believe I was yelling for help. Was I?"

"You mean to say, you don't know if you wanted help or not?" questioned the bird.

"Quite right" Caterpillar nodded. "Sometimes when I am deep in contemplation I forget myself. I get so caught up in information."

"Your brow is rather wrinkled, Caterpillar. What are you in contemplation about?" asked the ever curious Alice.

Caterpillar pointed out the large leaves he was holding in one hand with the nozzle of his pipe he held in the other. "Do you see these? This is the result of the research I conducted regarding our consumers—the folks who drink our teas. I have conducted interviews of many groups of tea drinkers."

Penguin squinted his eyes, but all he could see were big, green leaves, nothing else. It seemed to him Caterpillar was reading tea leaves. Was there actual information there or was it simply in the consultant's imagination? He looked at the leaves from many different angles, but his conclusion remained the same: no information was visible. "What exactly do you have that you can tell us?" questioned the bird, disbelief evident in his voice.

Alice raised her eyebrow at Penguin to caution her friend against teasing Caterpillar. He seemed to understand her signal and adjusted his tone. "What information have you gathered that can help us?"

"Well, you see, I have discovered something that causes me some discomfort." He paused and he took a puff from his pipe. Obviously the habit allowed him to study things closely and lessen his discomfort, which is why there had been so many smoke rings.

"Go on, please, Caterpillar" said Alice encouraging him to continue.

"We have always had a very loyal following of tea drinkers. They have loved our teas. They have told us so many times and proven it to us by purchasing more and more of it. In truth, they purchase as much as we can produce."

He continued seeing he had a captivated audience. "They like the names, the tastes, the packaging, the quality. "

"So far, that sounds very good, Caterpillar" Alice confirmed.

"Yes, it is, Alice. But lately things have started to shift. Our sales are falling and I wanted to know why. They have written to us complaining our quality has decreased. Our flavors are less distinct. They are confused by our packaging. But, Alice, we haven't changed anything. Nothing! Nothing at all!"

"I can see why that's distressing, Caterpillar. It doesn't make any sense." Alice told the consultant.

"And how can we stop something if we don't know what it is

we are trying to stop?" piped up Penguin.

"Precisely! That is why I decided to invite some drinkers to my haven to question them directly. "

"You did that on your own, Caterpillar?"

"Alice, that's what Leaves-of-Wonderland hired me to do: to act independently of the company as an outside consultant, to help when the business needs help."

"Why, that's very nice and helpful, Caterpillar. Thank you."

"Yes, yes" declared Penguin, unable to hide his impatience, "So, did you discover anything?"

"Yes, I did" said Caterpillar proudly. "It seems our customers are confused. They are confusing our Leaves-of-Wonderland Tea blends with another tea. This other company is producing teas very similar to ours in name and packaging, but the quality is far inferior to ours. And it is cheaper. The tea purchasers thought we were producing a cheaper line, or worse that we decided to lower the quality of our teas, producing them cheaply with cheap ingredients and cheap processes. Therefore, folks are turning to other brands for their tea satisfaction."

"But, Caterpillar, we are not doing that!" said Penguin, emphatically.

"That's true, Penguin, but the public doesn't know that."

"Hmm" thought Alice aloud. She recalled her earlier exchange with her feline spy. "Cheshire Cat was right. This competitor is doing this to us on purpose. They want to steal our good name and our customers. The foreign competitor he hinted at is behind all this."

She turned to Penguin. "My dear, Penguin, there seems to be more to this story than we may have originally believed. We must push on and make everything right. Not only for Leaves-of-Wonderland but for our loyal following. Without our customers we have no business!" She was distressed, who wouldn't be, but she was resolute that Leaves-of-Wonderland required her assistance now more than ever, and she knew in her heart she would do whatever it took to regain her company's good name.

She faced the consultant. "Thank you, Caterpillar. It's not good news, but I am glad we now have more of the whole picture." And with that declaration, Alice gathered her courage and readied herself to leave. "Excuse us. We must make haste. Caterpillar, we'll leave you to further conduct your research while we pursue some remedies to our great mess. Good bye."

WORKBOOK
11 A SMOKEY OMEN

SUMMARY

Puff! Puff! Alice and Penguin are once again thrown off course, this time by the strange sight of smoke rings rising in the air. Are they a mystical message? Are they a signal to someone? Where there is smoke, there is fire, and therefore someone might need help. Alice pulls Penguin with her and they rush to discover what is wrong. Alas! Upon reaching the smoke's source they discover the rings are caused by Caterpillar puffing on his hookah, deep in contemplation. He is so deep in thought he doesn't realize anyone could see his smoke rings furthermore surmise they are either a coded signal to someone or, worse yet, an alarming fire.

With some questioning, Alice and Penguin learn from the consultant the root of his concern: there is a problem with customer satisfaction. The once loyal drinkers of Leaves-of-Wonderland were defecting! In an effort to discover why, Caterpillar had conducted his own research by gathering data from tea drinkers. What he learned isn't pleasant…

It seems there is a competitor who is imitating Leaves-of-Wonderland's packaging and flavor names, but of a poor quality and at a cheaper price. Unsuspecting consumers have been duped into buying the inferior teas, assuming they were Wonderland products when in actuality it was a bit of trickery perpetrated by a shrewd foreign rival. (This was in line with what Alice had learned earlier from Cheshire Cat).

Infuriating! This new information further enflames Alice's resolution to fight for her company. She thanks the consultant for his work then she and Penguin leave him to continue his research as they resume their trek.

WHAT ALICE LEARNED

- Paying attention to signals/warnings is important.

- Regardless of anything else, pleasing the customer is the essential purpose of the company because without customers, there are no sales.

- Being defensive doesn't help her solve anything.

    What other lessons do you see that Alice has encountered in this chapter?

    _____
    _____
    _____
    _____
    _____
    _____

DISCUSSION QUESTIONS

1. What change, if any, do you see in Alice? If you see a change, what do you think it means for her and the company?

2. Why does Caterpillar see things others in the company do not? How can Alice use this to her advantage?

3. What circumstances at the company have left it vulnerable for the foreign competitor?

SHORT ANSWER QUESTIONS:

1. As a hands-on leader, is it wise of Alice to delegate something as important as the continued customer research to Caterpillar?

    ___Yes   ___No

    Why did you select the response you did?

2. Has Alice (select one response)

    a. has gathered enough information and should now go confront Hatter and the Queen?

    b. should she continue on her quest for information to ensure she is well armed before confronting them?

3. Have you ever mistaken a product that was close to another brand, only to find out it wasn't the purchase you had intended?
   ___ Yes   ___ No

   If yes, what was the product?

   For future purchases, did you go back to the original product or were you happier with the replacement?

11.5 I SPY A MARKETING DEPARTMENT

Upon leaving Caterpillar, Penguin reflected on their situation and thought perhaps even more of the picture would come into view with a quick visit to the marketing department. "Alice, we should take a slight detour, if you don't mind." He posed the idea gingerly knowing she may not be open to the suggestion.

"Well," Alice began. "I was thinking we should visit the marketing department to uncover what they know about the competitor and its actions. That department, if it isn't already aware of this situation, should be alerted. Did you have the same thought, Penguin?"

"Precisely," he said, relieved.

"Where is Marketing? Is it far?"

"Actually, it's between Caterpillar's haven and the HR office. It's in some wetlands, however."

She laughed at herself recalling her earlier absentminded walk into the lake. "We've already gotten our feet wet walking into uncharted territory all day, what harm could a few more puddles do?"

They roamed in the direction Penguin had indicated until they entered a clearing overlooking a pond. At first, all was still, but then they saw the brilliant pink hue of movement. The movement was graceful, beautiful. They stood transfixed by the exquisiteness of the sight. As they drew closer, the pink feathers, black beak and long legs transformed into Flamingo. Penguin called ahead to the pretty bird. "Excuse me, are you the marketing department?"

The bird turned its head toward them. "I am at the moment. My two colleagues are taking their tea break, but someone has to hold down the department should any emergencies arise or someone come to visit." Flamingo took a good long look at Alice and Penguin trying to size them up before continuing, "Are you coming to propose a new label, a new flavor, a new name? Or-" she hesitated. "Are you here to complain about a label, flavor or name? Those are usually the reasons folks come to visit us. We are a popular department. Everyone has their opinions. What are some of yours?"

"Actually, we are not here to propose anything new or to complain about a particular taste not to our liking," Penguin informed her.

"Oh," the long-legged bird sighed, clearly disappointed. She was looking for insights from outsiders. "We haven't had a visitor in a while. No, no request for something new, something creative, something interesting. It's beginning to get a little dull around here. You know the taste kitchen had to cut its staff because of budget constraints, and ever since then we have to depend on customers and other visitors for new ideas. I've had nothing new come into our pond in a while."

That put a nasty idea into Penguin's head, which he voiced in an accusatory fashion. "Have you been so bored that you would tamper with some of the established blends? Or perhaps their names or labels?" Flamingo looked confused and affronted by Penguin's outrageous suggestion.

"Penguin, that's no way to talk to Flamingo. She may not have the knowledge we do about the Leaves-of-Wonderland issue we have learned of today." She turned to Flamingo's startled pink face, "We were alerted we have a competitor who is selling teas resembling ours but are not up to our high standards.,"

"Oh, surely, she knows that," rattled Penguin. "She has to be aware of our competition and our slipping customer base at all times. She keeps track of those details."

Flamingo shook the water off her back. "Yes, I keep informed. And I am aware we are losing customers, although I haven't been able to see a reason why. We haven't changed our packaging, ingredients or advertising. Frankly, it's been a good mystery. I will add, though, the slippage hasn't been noticeable enough to suggest any one cause."

Then she stopped to consider Penguin's words. "Wait a minute, are you suggesting I am somehow guilty of changing our existing teas without telling anyone or that I am contributing to that effort?"

"No, Flamingo" Alice said calmly. "We've just learned from an independent study our customers are being deliberately confused. We have a competitor that is selling teas similar in name to ours with similar but inferior flavorings and it's quite easy to get the tea choices mixed up. We don't have all the details yet, just some early findings. Is there anything you can tell us about this? Do you know any reason why this could be happening?"

Flamingo stared at her a moment before answering. "I know an Eastern competitor has produced such tea options. We've been following the numbers, but weren't aware that we've been losing tea drinkers because of their blends. So our customers believe they are actually drinking Leaves-of-Wonderland tea? And because they are dissatisfied with the taste they're giving up our brands of tea? Is that what you are saying?"

"Yes. That seems to be the case."

"Are you sure?"

"The study suggests this but we don't know how widespread it is," Alice stated.

Flamingo shook her head. "This is terrible! Perhaps we could change our labels and make them more difficult to imitate."

"That would only work for a while, Flamingo" offered Penguin. "What we really need to find out is who is behind this. Is there a leak somewhere?"

Flamingo's small eyes opened as wide as possible. She was clearly startled. "Why, why, uh, uh…"

"Obviously, by your surprised reaction, you don't know anything about this situation, Flamingo. But now you at least know of our state of affairs. Please tell your colleagues." She turned to Penguin. "Penguin, it's obvious Flamingo has no further information to share with us about the competition. Let's continue our original path and find our way to HR, perhaps that department might have some more clues to this and other things.

"We'll be on our way, Flamingo. We appreciate your help." Alice said and politely nodded her head.

Flamingo called after them. "Who should I say came by to tell the marketing department of this wrong-doing?" But Alice and Penguin were too far away to hear her.

Penguin was shaking his head, adrift in questions. Alice was determined to find answers and was deliberate in her strides toward the

HR department.

"What does she really know, Alice? Did that reaction of surprise seem genuine to you?"

"I don't know, but you seem to be asking some good questions, Penguin. Is it possible that there's a spy among us, particularly in the marketing department? For we didn't meet the other members."

Penguin stopped in his tracks and pivoted toward her. "Perhaps we should go back and wait for the others to return and question them too?"

"It's an interesting thought that we will have to add to our puzzle. However, we have other things to address and I don't wish to be side-tracked any further. Perhaps, there is no spy and it's merely a circumstance of very smart research. Let's move forward and see what happens. If there is a spy we will undoubtedly uncover additional clues, which will lead us in that direction. Meanwhile, at the moment, ours is a different direction."

WORKBOOK
11.5 I SPY A MARKETING DEPARTMENT

SUMMARY

Once again our intrepid friends are on the move. However, both of them feel that there is a missing link that needs to be connected: Marketing. After all, how can they truly understand the scope of the problems that have been laid at their feet if they don't know what marketing knows.

Upon their arrival, Alice and Penguin meet Flamingo, the lone representative of the department. It quickly becomes apparent that Marketing too is in trouble. The ennui that has impacted other parts of the company has also found its way here. Her comments indicate that Flamingo and her co-workers are lacking in purpose. This leads Penguin to wonder aloud if she or someone else could possibly have been so bored as to create problems in order for them to have something to do.

Alice and Penguin discover Flamingo is familiar with some of the purported issues involving Leaves-of-Wonderland. However, it seems the department is ignorant of the scope of the problems, and their potential for creating further havoc.

Or is she really that innocent? Could it be that Flamingo knows more than she has alluded to? Penguin and Alice are quick to depart, not wanting to divulge anything further until they can put the rest of the pieces in place.

WHAT ALICE LEARNED

- To think more strategically as evidenced by her desire to visit the marketing department to gather information.

- To be more confident and assertive with the departments.

- That it's much more important to gather information from an employee than it is to blame the employee or informant.

    What other lessons do you see that Alice has encountered in this chapter?

    _____
    _____
    _____
    _____
    _____
    _____
    _____

DISCUSSION QUESTIONS

1. In your opinion, what has contributed to the boredom that the folks in Marketing are experiencing? How does this translate into 'real world' situations?

2. In this chapter as well as in others, Alice negates something that Penguin has said in the presence of others. In this instance she says, "Penguin, that's no way to talk with this charming flamingo". Does she handle this in an appropriate manner? If no, how would you coach her to say it differently?

3. What additional information do you think that Alice should have tried to glean from her visit with Flamingo?

SHORT ANSWER QUESTIONS

1. Would you have visited the marketing department after discovering the competitor's strategies from Caterpillar's research or would you have kept to the original plan of going straight to Human Resources?

   ___ Yes   ___ No

   Is it a question of "staying on track" or "not sweating the small stuff"?

3. Do you think that there is a spy at the company?

   ___ Yes   ___ No

   What makes you feel as you do?

3. Was Alice too easy on Flamingo with her questioning?
   ___ Yes   ___ No

   Why or why not?

   Have you ever questioned someone in a superficial way because you didn't want to know the real answers, didn't care, or weren't willing to deal with the consequences because a decision would have to be made?

12 HR CAWING

Until their pow-wow with Caterpillar, the unfaltering duo had been totally engrossed in what was happening within the company. Now, however, they knew there were the added troubles of what lay outside the company as well. In fact, Penguin had been so walloped by Caterpillar's research results that he almost forgot Alice's immediate agenda as well as his own duties, until he saw a torrent of workers from a variety of departments all headed in the same direction, and it jolted him out of his trance.

"Alice, I didn't realize what time it was! I got lost in our discussions. I must leave you. There's a special party at Hatter's and I must be there! You see, we had to RSVP and I said I would go.

"That means you'll have to go alone to HR and after our conversation with Beaver, I know you can manage it. You've convinced me of that."

"Yes, but-" however, Penguin had already waddled away, leaving Alice alone. Strangely, Alice had not been invited to the party. Perhaps this was an oversight, perhaps it wasn't. Either way, she didn't have time to worry about it. She was too concerned about company business and HR to feel slighted.

Alice meandered toward HR, which while causing so much controversy also had a daunting aura surrounding it. She was doing battle with her fear, but wasn't at all sure if she was winning. In order to convince herself that she could handle whatever she found there, she repeated a mantra, "I can do this. I am the founder. It's just another department. It's a necessary action I have to take. I can do this."

Feeling better about the situation, she proclaimed "I am no

longer the child who started this day. I am wiser and I now come prepared with facts and knowledge . . . and confidence . . . and wits."

She briefly thought about Penguin and wished he were there with her for an additional supportive presence. Then she smiled at her realization. She had formed a strong bond with the well-dressed bird, and Beaver too. And in a way they both were there with her. "I also have allies. Yes," she said triumphantly. "Now I have allies. And with that realization, her meandering became a purposeful march forward.

She strode proudly until she reached a door with a very shiny brass knocker. At last, she had reached the home of HR. She grabbed the brass ring firmly in her hand and knocked three times.

She waited. There was no response. She tried again this time, knocking a little heavier. Again, she waited. Still no response from the HR department. After waiting for a reasonable amount of time—she was trying to be careful, patient and polite—she opened the door a crack and peered in with one eye at what lay inside. "Hello?" She couldn't see anyone. She opened the door a little more to have a better view. There was no one inside. "Maybe I should wait inside for the HR representative to return." And that's just what she did. She entered the interior of HR and sat down on what looked like the right place to plant herself. And she waited.

While waiting, she took a keen look at her surroundings. "This place seems to be built like a nest with twigs and string, paper, pencils, leaves, but, there are a lot of shiny things here, too. Let's see, there are bells and whistles. There are coins, medallions, and shiny ribbons. Someone here certainly likes to collect sparkly things!" After Alice's survey of her environment, there was nothing left to do but wait for "the someone" to arrive. Then she had a brilliant thought, "Oh, perhaps the HR someone is at Hatter's gathering? In that case, I may have to wait a while. Maybe there's a better place to wait where I might be more comfortable with more shade. The sun is moving and pretty soon the glare on the things here will be blinding, and the direct heat will be intolerable. I also don't want to give HR the impression that I have been waiting here for a very long time. But I should let the HR someone know that I have been here and that I'm to be expected back." She loosened a pencil and paper from the nest and wrote: "Important! Will return soon. Alice."

With note in hand, she got up from her perch and posted it on the front door, anchoring it in place underneath the knocker's brass ring. She thought to herself, "This note could not possibly be missed now." She walked out the door and retraced her steps until she found a large tree. She sat in the shade underneath its lovely canopy and shut her eyes a while. It wasn't long before she had fallen asleep. She awoke sometime later, the sun in her eyes and a bird cawing above her.

"That was a good nap. I wonder how long I slept." She stretched. "Let me straighten myself out a bit. I don't want to visit HR appearing disheveled." She brushed the leaves from her hair and dress, stretched again and shook the cobwebs out of her head.

She returned to HR to find the note gone. She used the knocker expecting someone to respond. No one did. She tried it again with the same result. She figured someone was inside, so what was the issue? She pushed the door wide open to the surprise of the inhabitant sitting in the middle of the nest.

"How rude! How rude! Don't you knock?! Knock!" said a magpie with her beak half-full with strings and shiny things.

"Knock? I did knock—twice! And I also said I would be back so you shouldn't be surprised that I am here!"

"What? What?"

"What? What?" Alice replied, confused.

"What? Who? Who?" the bird twittered.

"First, I knocked twice and you didn't respond, which is why I opened the door. Second, I left a note on the brass knocker. It read, 'Important! Will return soon.' and I signed my name." There was a sharp tone to Alice's voice.

"Okay, you don't have to get huffy and puffy and all mighty with me! With me!" Magpie croaked.

"You're right, I don't. I will calm down."

Alice realized the bird repeated what she said twice. That was the way with magpies perhaps, or, was it just that the bird thought everything bore repeating so the words would carry more meaning. Or, perhaps she wasn't used to being listened to the first time she said something.

Alice felt bad that Magpie might have to say everything twice because her words weren't paid attention to. Alice started again. This time less forcefully. "But, you are in the wrong, you know. I left you a note, which I figure you must have read. It is in front of you after all. See?" She pointed to the note. "You removed it from the door so you must have read it."

"Oh, that. That."

"Yes, that! That!"

"And so, who's Alice? Alice?"

"You read it! Alice is me! Me!" In her frustration Alice was beginning to catch Magpie's habit of repeating her words. Then she caught herself. She didn't want Magpie to feel she was imitating or making fun of her.

"So, who are you? Are you?"

"I already told you. I'm Alice".

"Alice who? Who? You are making yourself sound like an important someone, so who are you? Who are you?"

"You don't know who I am?"

"No. No! Am I supposed to? Supposed to?"

"I'm the founder of the company, Alice Liddell."

"So, how come I've never heard of you? You? You can't be all *that* important. Important. That's why I ignored your note. Ignored your note," admitted Magpie. "I only answer to people I know. I don't have time for anyone else. Anyone else. I have way too much to do, and everyone thinks I report to them and work for them. Work for them."

Alice was beginning to get a picture of Magpie's world. She realized, not only did Magpie have to repeat herself to be heard, but everyone treated Magpie as if she was their own personal staff, which wasn't very nice. The bird seemed to be fair game as a target for everyone at the company. Alice realized that she was guilty of the same bad behavior. Why not explain things to Magpie and listen to the HR manager's story?

"To whom do you answer, Magpie?"

"To Hatter, Hatter and sometimes to the Queen. Queen. Hatter runs the company, you know. You know."

"Yes, I hired Hatter as President to oversee the company."

"You hired Hatter? Hatter?"

"Yes, as I told you, I am Alice, the founder."

"Alice, the founder of what? Alice, the founder of what?"

"Alice, the founder of Leaves-of-Wonderland!"

"*The Alice*!?" Magpie squawked.

"The very same!" said the girl, proudly.

"I thought she wasn't a real person. I thought she was a part of company legend. Company legend. A myth. A fairy tale. That's what

Hatter taught me. Taught me."

"Really?"

"Really! And the Queen of Hearts never said anything differently. Never said anything differently."

"Okay, it's not really important what you were told. You know the truth now. I am a real person. I am the person who started the company, who hired Hatter, who in turn hired you."

"I see. I see." said Magpie looking at her reflection in one of the many medals that adorned the nest.

"Yes, and then you made a lot of hires. And I must say, some of them are not very good."

"Not good? Good? Who are you to criticize my hiring? My hiring? Where were you when they were being interviewed? Being interviewed? You signed off on their employment. Their employment. Yes, all of the hires! All of the hires!"

"What do you mean? You mean the bad hires are my fault? I wasn't there making them."

"No, you weren't. Where were you? Where were you? You should have been here if they mattered to you. Mattered to you. So, yes, they are your fault! Are your fault!"

"Let me get this right. You hired them. I somehow signed off on their employment, which I don't remember doing. I am sure Hatter did that for me as the appointed President—"

"As the appointed President, you gave him the authority. You gave him the authority. And you haven't trained them, managed them, fired them, rewarded them, nothing. Nothing."

"And neither have you!"

"No, I haven't. I haven't been trained or given the authority to do those things. Those things."

"No wonder things are such a mess!" Alice said exasperated. What about Hatter? Has he been training them, managing them, firing them, or rewarding them?"

"No. No. The only thing he had me do was to write a book on policies and procedures. Policies and procedures."

"Yes, I've heard mention of this book from Manufacturing."

"I am surprised you have heard of it. Sadly, nobody seems to pay attention to it. But when I wrote it there was no one to give me feedback, so I wrote what I knew and then it became fact. Became fact. I was given the responsibility to write a book of procedures that no one ever reads. No one ever reads.

"Hatter told me I had to write about the operations of each department but didn't give me the authority to get information from each department head. Department Head. So, I did what I could. What I could". Magpie said forlornly.

Alice shook her head. The situation was beginning to become clearer.

"I am not here to ruffle your feathers." Alice said gently.

"You're not? Not? That's all you seem to be doing, Alice Liddell. Alice Liddell," said the offended bird.

"I'm just trying to understand the situation here after being away for so long. I'm sympathetic to your woes but I am trying to understand the whole story."

"So, ask me what you need to know if you truly want to understand how the company works. How the company works."

"Magpie, how do we pay our staff?"

"Each individual gets compensated depending on their preference. Puppy wants kibble. Duchess wants compliments and finery. Rabbit wants carrots, clocks and vests. Caterpillar wants tobacco and spices. You see? You see?"

"Everyone gets compensated differently? Wow! How on earth can you manage all that?"

Magpie shook her head. "It's not easy. It's a burden I have to bear given my duties".

"And how do they get rewarded if they are doing a good job?" Alice delved further.

"Hatter gave me these medals but he didn't explain how to give them and when to give them. So I kept them. Kept them. They look so good in my nest, don't they? Don't they? They're my reward, my reward, for having to do the best I can without much supervision or authority. Supervision or authority." Magpie thrust her neck out indignantly.

"But don't you understand, Magpie? They're not really yours. You didn't do anything to deserve them."

"I wrote the manual. I take the blame for everything that goes wrong with the company. Wrong with the company. Everyone complains to me. Everyone complains to me. I've never received one compliment from anyone. From anyone! I deserve a medal! I deserve many medals! Many medals!"

Alice felt badly for the poor bird. Magpie never received any good news, just demands and blame.

Magpie hid her head underneath her wing. She was ashamed of her job, ashamed that she had stolen the medals, but what was she to do at this company? She had no authority and no one really wanted to listen to her squawking.

"There, there, Magpie. I can see you are in a difficult position. We've covered a lot of territory today, but what about contracts and legal documents concerning hiring and employment? We didn't discuss that yet."

"We have a legal department. Legal department."

"I visited our so-called legal department. Do you know they spend the entire day studying for the bar? They never seem to be able to get past it. Consequently, the attorneys, if you can call them that, don't have the authority because they haven't passed the bar. They don't have the authority to sign, confirm, or negotiate anything."

"You mean nothing gets done in that department? Nothing gets done in that department?" said an outraged Magpie. "They are not doing their jobs? Their jobs?"

"That's right because they don't have the training or the official recognition. They only come to visit, hoping one day they will be given authority to help the company," explained Alice.

"So, they are a lot like me? Like me? Oh, this is not good at all, Alice!" Magpie shook her head and it banged into one of the bells nearby. It sounded off with a big "Bringggg!"

"Oh!" said Alice. "It sounds to me like you are doing the best you can." She wanted to encourage the HR manager. "Frankly, I am surprised you haven't left the company with all you're forced to endure!"

"I have. I have. But then I come right back. Come right back. I just can't seem to leave my nest. Leave my nest. It's become my home. My home." Magpie shrugged her wings.

"Magpie, I will try to solve some of these problems so you won't have to worry about them. I must talk with Beaver, my mentor, and Penguin, my assistant. Then, these things have to be discussed with Hatter. But I will resolve them. I have to or the business will collapse, and the folks who work here will be left without a job." Alice shuddered at the thought.

"I hope you can make things right. Things right. And if I can help you, tell me what I can do. What I can do. I am waiting for some direction. Some direction. I would welcome it. Welcome it!"

Alice smiled at Magpie. "I know, Magpie. You are a good bird! I know I can count on you for help if I need it. I promise to return with some answers. Meanwhile, you can keep the medals. You do deserve them." And with that, she left the nest.

Alice hurriedly retraced her steps with excitement. She couldn't wait to share what she had learned with Penguin.

WORKBOOK
12   HR CAWING

SUMMARY

Alice's confrontation with the HR department was about to begin. Yet, at this crucial time, Penguin must leave our heroine to attend a by-invitation-only tea party thrown by Hatter. Alice gathers her wits and summons her confidence approaching HR. She is prepared for a monster of enormous proportions, and is, therefore surprised to find an angry squawking Magpie as the HR representative.

Magpie, who has never met Alice, believes the tale Hatter has told her: Alice is merely a fable. When confronted with the truth, Magpie goes on a rampage about how mistreated and unappreciated she is. Alice accuses Magpie of making bad hires at the company, and the little bird throws that fault back on Alice because she should have been around to "sign-off" on the hires, but the CEO had flown the coop and was nowhere to be found. She also squawked at the CEO for forgetting to manage, reward, train and discipline the staff. Alice realizes she must try to make amends with Magpie. So, she draws on what she had learned from her earlier adventures that listening patiently allows her to gather information, and that asking the right questions can lead to some important answers.

With her change of approach, Magpie is more than willing to share information about pay, rewards, the company manual, contracts and legal documents concerning hiring. Magpie tells all once she realizes the CEO really does care about the company and the important job she has been doing. Alice is not like others that Magpie has had to answer to who blame everything on her and never leave a kind word behind. By the end of the conversation, Magpie trusts that she has found a supporter in Alice and Alice has a heck of a story to repeat to Beaver and Penguin. She leaves the beleaguered bird with supportive sentiments and promises to help and hurries off to find her "team".

WHAT ALICE LEARNED:

- Fear of the unknown is often worse than the reality of a situation.

- When you give a character a chance to vent their frustrations, they are often more amenable to listening afterward.

- Folks might be both happier on the job and do a better job if they receive positive feedback.

    What other lessons do you see that Alice has encountered in this chapter?

    _____
    _____
    _____
    _____
    _____
    _____

DISCUSSION QUESTIONS:

1. Have Alice's fears of HR and its impact on the company been realized? Why or Why not?

2. Is the CEO ultimately responsible for hiring? If not, who is?

3. What evidence of Alice's growth do we see in this chapter?

SHORT ANSWER QUESTIONS:

1. Do you feel Alice showed the proper respect for Magpie when they first meet?

   ___Yes ___ No

   Does Alice's behavioral change toward Magpie at the end of the chapter cause you to have second thoughts about how you initially viewed Magpie?

   ___ Yes ___ No

   Do you believe you would have been fair-minded with Magpie?

   ___ Yes ___ No

   Why or why not?

2. Who is the **biggest** culprit in creating the problems in HR? (Select best answer)

    a. Magpie
    b. Alice
    c. Hatter
    d. Penguin
    e. Duchess
    f. Queen of Hearts

3. What is the symbolism of Magpie repeating herself?

13 THE TRUTH REVEALED

As Alice was making her way back through the woods to Beaver's dam she thought, "All this time I was envisioning HR as some monster responsible for my woes, but the poor thing is just a frightened magpie. I feel she might be able to muster up some courage, now that we've spoken. If she can do that, Magpie could be instrumental in helping the team make the company into the success it once was and it can be again."

Alice was excited to rejoin her friends, and she hurried down the trail as fast as her feet would carry her. She had a great deal to share with her team. As she rounded the bend in the path she was surprised to see Penguin was already there, waiting for her. He was sitting on their favorite toadstool, watching the ever-industrious Beaver.

"Penguin," she exclaimed breathlessly. "I'm so glad to see you, although, I didn't expect you back from the tea party so soon. I have so much to share with you, but first tell me about the party. Did you have fun?"

Penguin simply stared at the stranger addressing him. "Excuse me. Do I know you?" he asked with an inquisitive tilt of his head. "How do you know my name?"

This odd question from her closest confidant rocked poor Alice back on her heels. What could it mean? Then she got the idea that Penguin was only playing a joke on her and she smiled. "Oh, I see!" she exclaimed. "You're teasing me. This is the disguise you wore to the party—pretending not to know me so that you could gather more intelligence."

"Young lady, I have no idea to what you are referring,"

responded Penguin. "I truly do not know who you are."

Hearing this interaction, Beaver paused in his work. He could tell from Alice's expression that she didn't know why Penguin was behaving in such a manner. It certainly appeared that Penguin genuinely did not recognize Alice. This was a startling development, and Beaver was wary of what it meant. "Do you know who I am?" inquired Beaver.

"Well of course I do," replied Penguin indignantly. "You are Beaver. Why would I not know who you are?"

"I thought that since you don't recognize Alice, you might not recognize me either," offered Beaver.

"Don't be absurd. The reason that I don't recognize this young lady is that I have never laid eyes on her in my life. You, my dear Beaver, I saw just a short time ago as I was on my way to Hatter's tea party. We stood right here on this very spot and spoke. Surely you remember?" Penguin was beginning to wonder why his friend was behaving in such a peculiar manner.

"Surely, Penguin, *you* remember that there was another party with us when you and I spoke?" exclaimed Beaver.

"Well," admitted Penguin, "I do have some remote recollection that there was someone else here when we talked, but frankly that person must have made no impression on me because I don't remember them."

"But Penguin, it was I who was there when the two of you were talking," cried Alice, as Beaver nodded in agreement. "What has happened to you that you don't remember me? I'm Alice and you are my trusted assistant. We spent the entire morning together visiting different departments. Please, Penguin, try to remember," she pleaded.

"Alice?" asked Penguin in a very small voice. He thought for a few seconds, and then a look of recognition came into his eyes. Alice was relieved. Whatever had caused her friend's amnesia had passed. However, the recognition she saw in his face was, in fact, Penguin remembering what Hatter had said. Penguin expressed with certainty. "Alice doesn't really exist. Today at the tea party Hatter told everyone how Alice was a character he created to be the symbol of the company. In fact, Alice is actually an acronym: A.L.I.C.E. Hatter says that every company needs an acronym."

"An acronym?" she demanded, her voice betraying her mounting anger. Not only was she angry, she was incredulous! How dare Hatter say she didn't exist and that her name was merely an acronym? With tightly clenched fists on her hips and her foot tapping in agitation, she asked in a controlled voice, "If I may, what does the acronym A.L.I.C.E. stand for?"

Penguin proudly exclaimed, "Always Live In Comfortable Excellence."

Alice replayed the words over in her mind and then declared, "That makes no sense at all!"

"But Hatter said-" began Penguin, sounding a bit less sure of himself.

"I don't care what Hatter said! I am Alice, and Alice is not an acronym. It is my name, and I am the founder and owner of this company."

As Penguin stared at her, his beak hanging open in surprise, Beaver confirmed what she had said. "It is true. I suspect you have been duped, my good fellow. Tell us about the tea party. Perhaps we can determine how you lost your facts."

Penguin recounted how he had gone to the tea party Hatter had invited him to. It was a get together to welcome new employees to the company. They had been served treats and tea that Hatter had announced was his own special blend. It was a particularly delicious tea, reported Penguin. Somehow it made him feel good—safe and trusting. He was particularly happy when Hatter had proclaimed that the tea would be available for free to every employee and that they should drink as much as they wanted. With this revelation, both Alice and Beaver understood what had happened to the poor chap—he had been tea'sed into false thinking!

"Oh my, this is terrible!" exclaimed Alice realizing the full implication of the situation. Soon there wouldn't be a single employee in all of Leaves-of-Wonderland who would know her. "Soon," she mourned, "everyone will believe that I'm nothing but a silly, meaningless acronym. What am I to do?"

"There is possibly only one antidote for this kind of poison," Beaver calmly stated.

"What is it?" pleaded Alice, desperate for any shred of hope that all was not lost.

"I'm afraid that you aren't going to like it."

"Whatever it is, I'll do it."

"Very well. The only potential antidote for this treacherous poison is the truth."

"The truth?" asked Alice, perplexed. "How can truth be an antidote for poison?"

Patiently Beaver explained that truth is the only way to dispel poisonous lies. "However, it isn't going to be easy," he added.

"What could possibly be easier than telling everyone I am Alice and that I'm obviously real?" she asked trusting that all would soon be right with the world again.

"My dear Alice, if it were that simple your friend and colleague here," he said, indicating Penguin, "would already remember you. It goes deeper than that."

Feeling quite frustrated with the entire situation, Alice demanded, "You said the truth was the antidote to Hatter's treacherous poison. Well, if I told the truth and that didn't work then you must be incorrect."

"You must tell the *whole* truth, Alice, not just the comfortable part."

The light of understanding slowly came to Alice. "You mean I not only have to proclaim who I am, but I also must confess my weaknesses and mistakes in order for people to believe me and be willing to follow me again?" Beaver nodded and a small smile spread across his face. "But won't that just make them less likely to recognize me because I will not look like a strong leader?" she inquired, a bit confused.

"So most people would think, but it isn't true. Your employees were ready to trust Hatter's tales because they were already uncertain of your existence before they drank his tea. Even Penguin, who knows you best, isn't sure. For people to follow you, you are going to have to convince them that you are real. For them to believe that you are real they have to trust you, and they need to feel that you care enough about them to be honest with them."

This gave Alice much to process. Until recently, she had been unwilling to peer into the looking glass at her own shortcomings. Now she was supposed to talk about them to her employees? Alice was unsure of this new development. "I'm not sure I like the idea of telling my employees about my mistakes. Perhaps there is another way?" She looked to Beaver to see if he would give her an alternative, but he had resumed his work on the dam.

After much internal debate Alice reluctantly said, "Very well, I will give it a try." With that she sat on a nearby toadstool so she could be at eye level with Penguin. She then proceeded to tell him about how she had neglected the company, and worst of all, taken her employees for granted. She apologized for not being a good leader, and promised that she would do her best to overcome her shortcomings. "To be honest though, Penguin, I cannot promise that I will be perfect. In fact, I know I won't be. For you see, I have much to learn in order to be a good leader. I hope you will forgive me and help me as I endeavor to do better."

After she had finished, she had to admit she felt much better. Even if her speech didn't have the intended effect, she was happy she had been honest with the one soul who had faith in her at a time when she hadn't even had faith in herself.

Much to her surprise, the look of recognition slowly returned to Penguin's eyes. He blinked, and it was if he had awoken from an enchantment. With a shake of his head, he dispelled the remnants of Hatter's toxic tea. "Alice, where did you come from and why are you staring at me?" It worked.

Alice was so happy to have her faithful friend back, that she hugged him. "What are we doing here? Hatter is trying to convince everyone that you don't exist. We must hurry," he said. "We have to stop him. You are real and everyone needs to know just how real you are."

With Penguin's keen mind restored, Alice and her friends devised a plan to stop Hatter's mad scheme to erase Alice from the memory of every employee.

WORKBOOK
13 THE TRUTH REVEALED

SUMMARY

When Alice arrives at Beaver's dam, she quickly receives a cold dose of reality when it becomes apparent that her closest ally no longer recognizes her. What had caused this sudden attack of amnesia that specifically erased Alice from his memory?

Upon further questioning, she and Beaver learn that Hatter had informed all who attended his party that Alice never existed. As he spread these treacherous lies, Hatter had graciously offered his guests as much of his special blend of tea as they desired. As they sipped the tea, memories of Alice grew fainter and fainter. Worse still, Alice learns that soon every employee in the company would be drinking Hatter's poisoned potion, and it would be as if she had never existed.

With his wise insights, Beaver is able to bring a sense of calm to this calamitous development. He explains to Alice that the only possible antidote for a poison such as this is the truth. Not just the 'tip of the iceberg' truth, but the whole truth. The kind of truth that is painful while being cathartic.

Alice doesn't much like this solution, but dislikes the alternative even more. Beaver assures her that admitting one's failings isn't a sign of weakness, but rather strength of character. Thus, she sits down with Penguin and bares her soul, confessing her shortcomings and her fears. She asks Penguin for his forgiveness and his assistance, even though, she admits, she will undoubtedly make many more mistakes in the future.

Slowly, the light of recognition returns to Penguin's eyes as he remembers Alice. At last, he is free of the effects of Hatter's tea. With that the three begin working on a plan to stop Hatter's mad scheme.

WHAT ALICE LEARNED

- There are different levels of truth. That which is on the surface may not be enough to build trust and loyalty.

- Showing one's vulnerabilities can be a sign of strength.

- Misinformation and gossip is toxic and anyone can fall victim to it.

What other lessons do you see that Alice has encountered in this chapter?

_____

_____

_____

_____

_____

_____

DISCUSSION QUESTIONS

1. Why do you think Penguin, who knows Alice better than anyone, would be vulnerable to Hatter's misinformation campaign?

   If you were Alice, after Penguin seems to regain his sense of self, would you have trusted him to remain that way?

2. How much 'truth' is enough for a leader to share with her team members in order to build trust and respect?

3. Why does Hatter want to erase Alice from the minds of the employees?

SHORT ANSWER

1. The saying "The truth shall set you free," is very apt here. Why is it so important for Alice to be honest if she wants people to 'remember' her? (Circle all that apply)

   a. She wants people to trust her
   b. She wants to gain sympathy
   c. It is difficult to be consistent when you are lying
   d. Without the truth, she seems shallow and unmemorable
   e. It draws upon common experiences so that employees will build a bond with her
   f. It makes her more human
   g. Other: _____

2. Beaver implies being open and honest is a sign of strength. Do you agree?

   ____Yes   ____No   ____Sometimes

   Why?

3. Beaver believes telling the whole truth is the antidote to Hatter's spiced tea. Is there another other antidote you could have suggested to Alice?

   ___ Yes   ___ No

   If so, what?

14 FISTICUFFS: DUELING POTENTATES

As Beaver, Penguin and Alice huddled together to coordinate their plans to attack Hatter's lies and evil tea ploy, Alice was able to see more and more glimpses of the real Penguin. She was gladdened by this discovery because it gave her hope she could turn a situation that seemed hopeless just a few minutes before, into something they could challenge and even hope to win. Beaver was also taking notice of the newly revitalized Penguin. He was happy to see the little fellow's animated personality returning.

"Alice, if I could turn on you after just a cup of that un-truth serum, can you imagine what will happen to the others who have never encountered you before?" The bird shivered.

"I experienced that already, with Magpie. She was convinced I was a legend, and she was at the same party as you. It all makes perfect, diabolical sense. That tricky Hatter! He is a mastermind."

"My better sense tells me, Hatter is not working alone, my dear girl. No, I sense he has support from another equally important figure that is emboldening him. Can you think of who that might be?" asked the straight-forward and wise Beaver.

She took a few minutes to ponder that question, and then started counting her facts on the fingers of her hands. "Well, it can't be Magpie, Puppy, Rabbit, or the legal birds, but it could be Cheshire Cat, Caterpillar, or Duchess. They're all smart and have been with the company long enough that they would have a loyal following."

Beaver interrupted. "Yes, they are all cunning creatures with history at Leaves-of-Wonderland, and they may be able to lure others into following them, but I don't think so. They don't carry the experience or immediate accepted gravitas of someone higher up. No, this is someone who is obsessed with power and control, and wants things their own way because they were born to the title. It's loyalty or perhaps more accurately royalty. Doesn't the Queen of Hearts control the board, Alice? And the board exerts its weight over Hatter, right?"

"It could also be the King," interjected Alice. "But he doesn't seem to have the need to control like she does. Unlike the queen, he would be happy spending his days playing croquet. Hmm, your idea makes sense. We know she has a strong personality and Hatter listens to her every want and wish because he's scared of her. Penguin, do you remember when we took our tea break in the woods today and caught him spying on us from behind a tree?" Alice was starting to put the pieces together and became excited by her problem solving discoveries. "Yes! Yes! And he couldn't run away from us fast enough once he noticed we'd discovered him there."

"And, Alice, he was running to a special engagement with the Queen, remember? That's what he told us," piped in Penguin.

"You know. I had blocked from my memory the original scenario that Cheshire Cat had used as a tease. He intimated that Hatter and the Queen were ganging up on me. Now, it all is coming together."

"Okay", said Beaver. "The two of them are laying the groundwork. They're building their own dam at Leaves-of-Wonderland. So, what to do about it?"

"Are Queen and Hatter drinking their own brew, Beaver?" She shook her head dispelling the thought. "Never mind. It really doesn't matter. What matters, just like with Penguin and Magpie, is that I have to confront them with the truth, whether or not they're drinking the doctored concoction. It has to be me and it has to be the truth coming from my mouth" said Alice, resignedly.

"I could come with you—to protect you." Penguin wanted to demonstrate his allegiance to Alice, being ashamed of his earlier behavior.

Alice put her hand on Penguin's shoulder and looked into his eyes. "I know you want to make things right after your evil-tea-laden comments. But, you see, this is a job that I must do alone. In order for Hatter to take me seriously I have to go at him alone, with no entourage, no magic tricks, just my wits and my confidence. If I can't face Hatter with my own words, how can I stick up for myself in front of anyone at the company? He is the key, and it has to be a fair fight."

"Alice, I am proud of you," Beaver said.

"I am as well," added Penguin. "I'm in awe of you being ready to take this big step, Alice."

"Thank you," she smiled at her comrades. "Whether I'm ready or not, I must do it. The future of this company relies on it, and for that reason alone I cannot back down. It's not just about me versus Hatter, it's about Leaves-of-Wonderland facing an unknown future. I am ready for this." She gathered herself together, preparing to start off on the lonely path leading to Hatter.

"Will you come find us after your altercation, Alice?" questioned Penguin.

Alice stopped to respond to her friend. "I hope there won't be an altercation, Penguin. I hope we'll just be able to have a discussion with an airing of our different viewpoints. That's my plan at any rate." She then continued walking, and quickly disappeared from their view.

Alice didn't have far to walk before she came upon Cheshire Cat who suddenly materialized in front of her. He grinned. "Where are you going?"

"Please excuse me, Cheshire Cat, I don't have time to chat." She scurried forward remembering their last unnerving encounter.

"Oh, so you know my name. I am at a disadvantage because I don't know yours."

Alice immediately understood that Cheshire Cat had sipped the tainted tea too and now they were at odds with their immediate agendas. She could see the countenance of the creature had altered; the inviting smile became a little guarded. It frightened her. Her pace quickened to escape the cat. She felt increasingly anxious. She must hurry to Hatter's. Time was slipping away quickly and there was none to spare. She knew she was being rude and creating further tension between them, but there was simply not enough time to parley with Cheshire Cat and accomplish her mission so she ignored the cagey feline and pressed forward.

The cat, realizing it had better things to do than speak to this stranger, vanished with its lasting smirk lagging behind, disappearing slowly into the air leaving Alice with an uncomfortable lasting impression.

Alice left the smile and quickly wound her way to Hatter's house. Arriving, she knocked at the door.

"No one's here." Someone replied. Alice knocked again.

"There's still nobody here!" replied the same voice.

Alice was becoming frustrated with the situation, and boldly turned the knob, opening the door. "Nonsense, of course you're in here, otherwise there wouldn't have been any answer. Now, what kind of game are you playing?" Alice demanded, her ire quickly increasing with the wily antics of Hatter. Without waiting for a reply or a proper invitation, Alice entered the house and slammed the door behind her. She stood looking at Hatter, her eyes narrowing as she glared at her adversary.

"What game would you like to play, Alice?" Hatter inquired coyly as he stood over a table, pouring tea for the last of the stragglers from the party.

"Well, at least you know better than to drink your own tea!" Alice said in an accusatory fashion. Hatter knew who she was even if the others had no idea.

"Oh, so it's going to be that kind of game? Well, then, I don't want to play. Can you find someone else? Maybe one of these characters would like to play with you?" directing her gaze to his guests. "Quite a few of them are very good at croquet." said the cheeky President. But of course, none of them knew who she was, nor did they care to know. They all ignored her, and continued chatting with each other, drinking their tea and eating dainty sandwiches.

"You are the only one I want to play with, Hatter."

"Okay, okay. Down, girl! Perhaps a cucumber sandwich may be just the thing to help you keep your cool".

Alice slapped the sandwich out of Hatter's hand. "I don't want a sandwich. You know why I'm here! I want answers!"

"Oh, now, now, please! We don't want to upset anybody, do we, hmm?" Then he addressed the others. "Can you all please leave me alone to deal with this young lady? You can take your sandwiches with you and there will be plenty more tea at another time. You can be sure. Now, please take your leave of us. Run along now, and thank you for coming!" The others quickly obeyed their leader and left with sandwiches in their hands, leaving their half-filled tea cups on the table. The last one to leave, a white mouse, closed the door behind him. The room suddenly became very quiet and empty, but was filled with the mounting anxiety of the two who remained: Hatter and Alice.

Now that the others had gone, Hatter set aside his playful

demeanor. His mood turned icy. He had been taken by surprise and he did not like it. "What's the idea of barging in like this, young lady?" Hatter was clearly irritated, feeling defensive. He had a sense that Alice was beginning to gather facts about the trap that he and the Queen of Hearts had so carefully laid. He hadn't anticipated that she was going to learn about their plan so quickly. He had taken all the logical precautions. How could this have happened? He had even invited Penguin to their little gathering and the assistant had sipped the spiked tea. Who else could have told her? Surely, it wasn't the pesky bird?" Hatter's thoughts were overwhelming him.

Alice sat down on one of the upholstered chairs in the dining room. She was looking at the crystal punch bowl, which was engraved with the letters: H.R.H.Q.H. It was filled with the spiked tea. H.R.H.Q.H? Her Royal Highness Queen of Hearts! Proof that the two were in this plot together.

"Alice?"

The girl gathered her thoughts and blurted them out. "Hatter, I know that you are plotting with the Queen. I know that you are trying to turn the staff at Leaves-of-Wonderland against me. I know the tea that you have been offering to everyone is laced with a special ingredient that causes everyone to be blinded to my existence, so that no one will recognize me as Alice, the founder of the business. You can't deny this. I've seen it with my own eyes. Prepare to defend yourself."

"Oh, I see. Sssso, who let the cat out of the bag? Penguin, that *loyal* assistant of yours?" Hatter felt cornered. He had thought he could squirm out of the situation but it was obvious the girl knew too much. He had thought he could deny his plotting, but now he had to take a different strategy: he would start by admitting it all.

"So, you are not going to deny it?"

"No, my dear. There's no reason to. You obviously already know the facts and my intentions were only for the best of the company," declared Hatter. Hmm, he thought. This discussion could be quite delicious. Maybe he could relish it after all.

"Your intentions? For the best of the company? Are you mad?" It was like a scene with Magpie. Alice found herself repeating Hatter because she was so incensed about his belief that what he was doing was for the good of the company. That couldn't possibly be!

"Alice, Alice, Alice. You haven't exactly been the model for a leader, have you?"

"No," she agreed.

"And you haven't exactly been around to follow the progress of the company, have you?"

"No."

"And you haven't been around to oversee the company, manage the hiring, write the procedures, reward the staff, communicate with the staff, change rules, manage unruly creatures, promote the good ones..." Hatter was going on and on and Alice was losing track of her shortcomings until he came to a proper halt. "..advise me?" She had shaken her head to all of his accusations because they were true. "Ah, so you see, you've been an absent leader. In fact, you haven't been a leader at all!"

"If you put it like that, I can't disagree." she said rather reluctantly.

"And how can I be expected to do my job without communication and direction from the person who hired me to lead the company? Where was I to go? What was I to do? I didn't know. There was no one for me to turn to, so I took it upon myself to do the best I could without your support, with the help of the Board. And, well the trouble is, young Alice, your company is not doing very well. No, not very well at all. I saw that if we didn't do something drastic, not only would the business go bankrupt, but the staff would lose their jobs and the beautiful business you built would simply cease to exist." He was preying on her emotions, trying to make her feel guilty.

He continued to explain his actions. "So, I discussed things with the Queen and King of Hearts and the rest of the Board. We had received offers to buy the company from some tea producers in Eastshire. The Queen and I thought that was the best possible scenario for the company and its legacy—to sell it. We are in talks with two possible contenders."

His tone changed from being matter of fact to being accusatory. "This was all fine and easy, when out of the blue, you decide to show up again. And you created havoc amongst the departments you visited. Yes, I am very aware of your comings and goings today. I heard you and Penguin in the woods. But, you see, Alice, we knew that you could possibly get in the way of our plans. So we took action to prevent it. Queen, Duchess and I concocted a tea that erased your existence from the memory of the staff. And without you to foil our plans, the sale would move forward."

"Duchess was in on this?" cried Alice.

"She knows who butters her bread in the end, my dear."

"No wonder she moved me out of the quality kitchen so quickly!"

"Can you blame her, Alice?"

"Hatter, I've learned a lot today about what's going on at Leaves-of-Wonderland. It appears to me, you are running the business into the ground purposely so you can profit from the sale, and you assume the only way to save it now is to sell it. I don't believe we were doing as poorly as you say until quite recently."

"Tsk, tsk, my girl. That's your opinion, and you are entitled to it. But I'm the one who has been here looking after things, not you. And because of that, I know what's best for Leaves-of-Wonderland." He took a few minutes to let his words linger and then hit her with a bigger punch. "Remember who hired me? Remember who was gone from the fold? You can't be an absent owner and then just slide in and expect everyone to listen to you and want to follow you. Leadership is not something that is granted automatically, you have to earn it. And how have you earned it, Alice? Oh, that's right, you haven't."

Alice considered his harsh words and struck back. "What's best for the people, or what's best for you and the Queen? What tidy sum do you tend to gain if a sale goes through, Hatter?"

"Oh, but as the majority owner, you would gain a lot too, Alice. Don't you see? Even without my special tea, everyone would think you wanted to sell because of the money you would make and that's why you haven't been around—because you really don't care about the business."

"Who says that, Hatter?"

"Well, I for one would, and I wouldn't mind telling everyone that. And everyone would believe me because your actions speak louder than your nice words, Alice." He grinned at her maliciously.

"Maybe you want what's best for the company and maybe you want what's best for you."

He interrupted her. "Can't they be one and the same?"

She continued. "I am going to fight this."

"How will you do that when no one knows who you are, my dear? Just go away quietly and let things be. Let the sale go through, earn your money, be happy our brands will still exist, just under a different company name. I bargained that caveat with both buyers. You have created a legacy and you won't have to run things. Now doesn't that sound…peachy?"

Alice explained to him some words of wisdom that she had learned. "You might trust that the buyers will agree to those things, but I bet when you sign on the dotted line and collect your money, this caveat will not be in the contract. A buyer will lure you with money and then change the terms at the last moment so that it works to their advantage. You can't possibly know that they will keep the same brand names as the ones we have. Under a new owner, everything is subject to change including firing and hiring. You don't think they will keep our staff, do you? No, they will put their own people in the positions and create their own identity. After all, it will become their brand and their legacy. It will probably not resemble Leaves-of-Wonderland at all."

"You think you're so smart, little girl. How do you know this?" Hatter was becoming increasingly uneasy with the conversation. He was having second thoughts about his entire strategy, but he had come too far to back out. He could taste the rewards that would be his. But Alice proved to be a bigger obstacle than he had ever foreseen and a smarter one. Damn, the girl!

"Well, Hatter, there was a time that I was approached by a buyer. I never told you and the Board about it, but I considered it. I seriously considered it. My family wanted me to sell, they said a tea business would never be profitable and a young girl should be playing and not running a company. I thought about all the things that could change with a new owner and I just couldn't do it. I couldn't do that to what we've all worked so hard for: the teas would change, the staff would change. And what would be left?" She was pleading her case.

"That sounds like a good tale, Alice. But, why then did you not stay and run the company like you should have. Your story doesn't add up to much."

"I was very young. My family had heard about the tea game, and thought it was a make-believe tale I had invented. When I started to take the game seriously, they became worried. They convinced me that a perfect compromise would be for me to hire someone to run the company, and I could then go learn my lessons, read, play dress-up, and do all the others things little girls do.

"As I grew, I realized that my family led me astray because they never understood that the business was real and not a figment of my imagination. I took the wrong advice from the wrong people, but I didn't know that at the time.

"I thought it was the right thing to do then, but I've had regrets seeing what the business has come to."

Hatter felt the sting of those last words as a direct accusation. He didn't like it. "Alice," he declared, while lifting his chin in an attempt to snub her and to add weight to his words. "I've made my decision. It is for the best. If I can't convince you, then I'll just have to fight you, if you make it into a duel."

"Will you fight fair, Hatter? Will you tell the truth? Will you still use your tea against me?"

"I will use whatever it takes to save jobs, and keep the business going."

"Hatter, I can't say if you are a liar, but you are certainly a coward. There is another choice: You can stand up to the Board if the Queen is behind this plan. You can stand up to any potential buyer. You can help turn this company around." Alice held a ray of hope that she could return him to reason.

"To turn it around, would take too much effort. It's too far gone, Alice. And, yes, the Board is strongly in favor of selling."

Her ray of hope had been extinguished. She quickly changed strategies. "Then I will use whatever it takes to make sure this doesn't happen. Lest you forget, I am the majority stockholder in this company and I won't agree to sell."

"Not even if you don't have a choice? My, you are a proud girl! You can't turn the company around, it will be too difficult."

"Perhaps, perhaps not, but at least I am willing to try! I am not giving up without a fight." She turned around and walked toward the door, her head held high.

"You are not making things easy for yourself or for others, Alice."

"Maybe not, Hatter, but I feel the company is worth fighting for and obviously you don't! That is the difference." She opened the door and closed it behind her. The match had begun, but it was not going to be an easy one and it may not even be a fair one.

The discussion with Alice left Hatter thoroughly confused, and he had to admit that he was not ready for the duel he knew was coming. Worst of all, he dreaded having to break the bad news to the

Queen. Unconsciously, he rubbed his neck with his boney fingers, imagining how she would explode when she learned of this development. Hatter was quite attached to his head and certainly didn't want to find it on her chopping block. Thus, he had to proceed cautiously. In spite of how he had appeared earlier, Hatter was not feeling at all confident, and wished that he had an ally who would lend him support and affirm his reasoning like that pesky Penguin did for Alice. Unfortunately, he was left alone to face the Queen's wrath.

What made Hatter even more uncomfortable was that he had to admit that Alice's arguments had merit. The plan didn't seem quite as wonderful as it had when the Queen recruited him for her mad conspiracy to sell the business. And, why did the Queen want to devalue the company by making it less profitable? Was it because the company was overvalued before as a result of its strong products, branding, and founder allure and no buyer could be found to pay the market rate? Or was it for some other unknown selfish reason? Oh, what to do? What to do?

As Hatter grappled with what these developments meant to him and his lovely head, he groaned. "Alice has so much moxie and fight in her. How could I have so underestimated her? I assured the Queen she wouldn't make a fuss. How could I have been so wrong? Yet, how could I have known she would return having been away from the company for so long?"

WORKBOOK
14 FISTICUFFS: DUELING POTENTATES

<u>SUMMARY</u>

As the three allies strategize about their next steps against the dastardly Hatter, Penguin poses the question that needs to be asked: How could he so easily forget his friend and leader after only one cup of the poisoned brew? Surely, this isn't a plan that Hatter could perpetrate on his own. After due consideration, they all agree that it has the signature of the nefarious Queen of Hearts all over it, and unless the plot is stopped quickly, it will be too late.

With that, Alice musters her courage to face Hatter on her own. After all, if she lacks the courage to stand up to Hatter and the Queen, then how can she expect her employees to have enough faith to follow her?

When Alice meets Hatter face to face, he is surrounded by the evidence of his deception, and he appears to almost enjoy the confrontation. The accusations of Alice's indifference and lack of leadership easily roll off his tongue. Alice realizes, Hatter is telling the truth. Yet, she cannot accept that his actions were all for the benefit of the company as he claims, and she challenges him.

For his part, Hatter is more than a little surprised at how insightful and informed Alice appears to be. This is quite a different Alice than he has become accustomed to, and he is taken aback by her parrying jabs at his logic. Some of her points even have him questioning his own plot. However, he refuses to allow her to see any cracks in his façade, and so continues to fight.

WHAT ALICE LEARNED

- Taking emotion out of conflict and simply using facts is the best way to present one's argument.

- Many people do not like conflict and will avoid it at any cost.

- You can't plan for every obstacle you may face.

What other lessons do you see that Alice has encountered in this chapter?

_____
_____
_____
_____
_____
_____

DISCUSSION QUESTIONS:

1. It is easy to consider Hatter the villain in this story, but is he really?

What do you think of his strategy and his motives?

2. The way the encounter between Alice and Hatter occurred escalated the animosity between them. This means there is little chance for compromise. What can Alice do as a next step that might help diffuse the conflict, and gain Hatter's support?

3. As the Chairman of the Board of Directors, what role *should* the Queen of Hearts play in determining the future of the business? What motives might she have?

SHORT ANSWER:

1. What positive attributes do you feel Hatter possesses?

2. If you were an employee of Leaves-of-Wonderland, who would you trust to have the best intentions for the company, and who would you follow?

   ____ Alice   ____ Hatter   ____ Queen of Hearts   ____ None are convincing enough yet

3. What motivates Hatter's relationship with the Queen? (Circle all that you feel apply)

   a. Fear
   b. Awe
   c. Friendship
   d. Politics
   e. He has a crush on her
   f. Common desire to do what is best for the company
   g. Common desire to do what is best for themselves
   h. Other _____

15 GATHERING STEAM

After her interview with Hatter, Alice was more resolute than ever. There was a determination in her that had been intensifying all day, much like a seedling in a hurry to break through the crust of the earth on its journey to meet the welcoming warmth of the sun. The meeting with Hatter had been the combustion that had sped up her growth. With every step she took, Alice could feel a mounting strength.

Alice rounded the curve in the path which brought her to the place where she had left Penguin and Beaver. After reuniting with her friends, she blurted out the very words that had been playing in her mind. "I am the founder and CEO of this company. No one is going to treat me like some cute little imaginary icon. I exist and I will not have my employees, nor the public told otherwise."

Beaver and Penguin both stood and stared at Alice, neither knowing quite what to say. Finally, Beaver slapped his tail on the ground to applaud her. "Well said, my dear. It is good to see you so determined. From your demeanor, I take it your interview with that rapscallion Hatter didn't go as you had hoped."

"No it didn't," replied Alice frowning. "He is incorrigible," she exclaimed in exasperation as she flopped down on a nearby toadstool.

"What are you planning to do next?" asked Penguin.

"I must convince all of my employees that I'm real. As we know, the only antidote for the tea is truth. Thus, it is high time I stir up a big batch of truth and deliver it to my employees." Alice looked up to see her friends regarding her skeptically. Understanding their concern, she laughed and reassured them by saying, "Oh, I don't intend to develop a truth tea. No, my dear friends, I am going to do something much more difficult than that: I am going to talk with them directly."

Her two allies breathed a collective sigh of relief.

"What are you going to say to them?" Penguin asked.

Alice paused for such a long time that Beaver and Penguin both thought she had not heard the question. Finally, she replied, her words coming slowly as she formulated her thoughts. "As I see it, there are a few things that I must convey to my team immediately. I must tell them who I am so that they can see there really is an Alice. Then I must apologize for not being quite present in my own company. But most importantly, I must tell them about the difficulties we are in, and share my vision for turning things around."

"Do you think that will work?" asked Penguin, a tinge of fear evident in his voice.

"No, I don't," she responded.

"Then why don't you do something different? Why do something you don't think will work?" cried Penguin, the worry in his voice rising.

"Alice is absolutely correct, it will not work. However, she has more, don't you my dear?" asked Beaver with a knowing look.

"Yes I do, Beaver. You see Penguin, simply telling the employees the truth won't be enough."

"It was enough for me. I didn't know who you were and I regained my memory when you told me the truth," argued Penguin.

"Of course you did my friend, but you had spent time with me and you had already begun to have confidence in me. No one else has had that experience."

As she finished, a dawning look of comprehension crossed Penguin's face and he said, "The first dose of the antidote will be to hear the truth, and then that must be followed up by seeing you in action. Is that right?"

"That is exactly right, Penguin! For the cure to be permanent, they must see I'm not just talk. I will do what I say I will do. If they do not see that, the effects of the poison might just well be permanent and all will be lost," confirmed Alice. Looking at her, Alice's friends knew she was determined to fight to regain her rightful place in the company.

Beaver saw a shadow of something else in her eyes, which he couldn't quite define. "There's something else isn't there?" he asked almost in a whisper.

"Yes," Alice replied. "I've been wondering how Hatter was able to develop a tea that would cause the ailment we have witnessed, 'Alice Amnesia', and I may have the answer." She paused, and her audience fidgeted, impatient for her to continue. "It was easy for him to accomplish. You see, I gave him the recipe."

"What!" her friends gasped in unison.

"What are you saying?" asked Penguin as Beaver cried, "How can this be?"

Alice calmed them down and replied, "All he had to do was to find a formula that would create the same effect as my own laissez-faire attitude." Seeing the confusion on their faces, she continued, "You see I had forgotten who I am almost as completely as those who had drunk Hatter's tea. I forgot my role and responsibilities to the company. Sure, I remembered my title, but certainly not what it meant. Now that I understand, I must help the others before it is too late."

And so, Alice and her two closest allies began planning how she was going to deliver the antidote. After a time, they had devised a plan they believed would work and were ready to set it in motion. They waved their goodbyes and set off to complete their assigned tasks.

The trio knew there were several people who had not succumbed to the effects of Hatter's tea. Alice's task was to reach out to them and convince them to help. She needed their assistance to bring the poisoned employees to Wonderland Clearing at the appointed time.

The first on her list was Duchess. Penguin had protested when Alice had mentioned her earlier, for Duchess had been part of the team of alchemists who had developed the treacherous tea. But Alice assured him that she would be careful, and her gut told her that Duchess could be swayed to come over to their side.

Alice approached Duchess' kitchen. The woman was closing the door when Alice slipped her foot in the crack right before it jammed shut. "Excuse me!" Duchess said crossly. "I was just trying to keep a pest out of my kitchen. What can Quality Control do for you today, young lady?"

Alice smiled her warmest smile, hoping to beguile the odd woman. "My dear, dear Duchess, you are the best at testing Leaves-of-Wonderland's products, ensuring that we never ship anything but the best to our customers. Because of this, I need your help."

Duchess, like most people, loves to receive praise and she felt certain that the praise offered by the young woman before her was genuine. "Thank you. Of course you are correct. This company would never survive without me. Who else could reign with such majesty over this kitchen? It's only too bad no one understands that."

"I understand it, Duchess. That's why I'm here," assured Alice.

"Perhaps," replied Duchess, looking somewhat pacified, "but who are you? You're not important! Until the people at the top recognize I'm important this company will never thrive."

"Surely you know me, Duchess? We spoke earlier today."

Confusion passed over Duchess's face as she tried to sort through the mixed messages her brain was sending. Her eyes took a deep penetrating look at the young woman before her and scrutinized her fair features. "It is true that you look familiar..."

Her voice trailed off as she noticed Alice looking at the table behind her. It was full of a variety of odd looking containers and devices, each of which was labeled with large letters and a series of numbers. Alice took a couple steps closer to the table out of curiosity, but Duchess quickly blocked her advance. "You are not allowed to see that—it is none of your business," she proclaimed with great authority.

"Why ever not?" asked Alice.

"Because it is a secret recipe, which I helped my wonderful President to develop. All of these are the different formulas I tested."

"I see," replied Alice, and truly she did. She saw that as a result of testing all the various concoctions, Duchess herself had become quite confused.

Alice gently led the woman to the large kitchen table that served as the conference room for the quality control department. Once there, Alice guided Duchess to the chair at the head of the table. Taking the chair at her right-hand side, Alice proceeded to tell her the truth. The light of recognition and clarity slowly replaced the confusion that had clouded Duchess' mind. "Do you know what this means?" demanded Duchess.

"What does it mean?"

"It means that that louse Hatter has used me as a pawn in his scheme."

"Surely, you knew what he was up to when he asked for your assistance," Alice replied skeptically.

"All I knew was that he and the Queen of Hearts hatched a scheme to take over the company. Frankly, I was all in favor of that because you were no more than a tale to most people around here. We hardly ever saw you or heard from you, and when we did, you didn't recognize us. We figured you didn't care about us or the company anymore."

Clearly, Duchess was not afraid to be blunt. She wasn't going to hold her tongue in order to protect Alice's feelings. Alice's instinctive reaction was to snap out a cruel response, but her better judgment prevailed. After all, weren't these the very things she had hoped for? Recognition and truth. The very least she could do was accept it humbly and gratefully.

"You are absolutely correct in your assessment of my behavior," Alice responded. As she said these words, she saw the fight had gone out of Duchess. She no longer wore the defensive visage she had sported moments earlier. Clearly, she was taken aback by Alice's honesty. "I know I have let you down, Duchess, and I hope you will give me another chance. Please, help me set things right. The company's future depends on it and I can't do it without you."

Duchess' enormous head grew with Alice's words. It was evident she wanted to be needed and respected—and who doesn't? "Very well then, tell me how I can help," she said. And the two put their heads together to plan their next steps.

After their conversation, Alice left Quality Control feeling stronger and more confident. She knew that she now had a mighty advocate in Duchess and she was feeling good about how she had gained the woman's trust and support.

After leaving Duchess' kitchen, she hurried to visit Magpie in HR. However, when she entered, Magpie surprised her with a loud squawk of disapproval.

"I'm sorry. Did I frighten you?" Alice asked.

Regaining her composure, Magpie nodded her head. "You can't imagine the things that have gone on here today. You wouldn't believe it! Wouldn't believe it! Why, there must be a crow in every tree, just waiting to pounce on some poor unsuspecting soul. Unsuspecting soul. It is getting more and more difficult to know who to trust around here! Trust around here."

"I'm sorry Magpie," sympathized Alice. "It must be unbearable for you."

"You have no idea. No idea!"

"Magpie, do you remember me?" Alice inquired.

"Of course I remember you! Remember you!" exclaimed Magpie, irritation evident in her voice.

"I didn't mean to insult you, but there are strange things afoot here today." Alice paused to collect her thoughts. She didn't want to ruffle the sensitive HR director's feathers any more than she had already done. Alice extended an olive branch, "Magpie, I need you to be my partner in making Leaves-of-Wonderland the best place to work. It won't be easy, but I promise you won't be out on a limb by yourself any more. Human Resources is too important to be treated as you have been." Alice paused to allow her words to sink in.

"Why should I believe you now? Believe you now? I have been here all along, willing to work together, but everyone just used me. Used me! What has changed? Has changed?" demanded Magpie.

"I have changed. You know that from our earlier discussion and what I have already confessed to you. I also believe that you want to be a partner in turning this company around and welcome the opportunity to have your talents and insights recognized. And not just with some bright, shiny trinkets, but with real authority where you can make a difference!"

Magpie played these words over and over in her head. It was true. She longed to be considered a valued partner, not just a silly clerk feathering her nest. If Alice was telling the truth, Magpie would finally get what she wanted. "Very well, I do truly want to be a partner! So, tell me what you need from me."

And just like that, Alice had her second ally.

***

While Alice had been winning over the Duchess and Magpie, Penguin had been busy with plans to gather all the employees in Wonderland Clearing. The trio had agreed that in order to get everyone to come they would have to make it very attractive to the employees. The WIIFM (What's in it for me?) virus was spreading through the company, and had everyone feeling rather down. As a result of this terrible virus, absenteeism had doubled, and the employees didn't seem to care about anyone but themselves. This was a terrible symptom of the ambivalence of Alice's inattention to the company and Hatter had allowed to flourish.

After much stewing, Penguin finally stumbled upon the solution to combat the WIIFM virus so that he could entice the employees to Wonderland clearing. Penguin decided to make the gathering a party to celebrate the employees. He would send word through the grapevine that everyone should meet to be recognized for their hard work.

Penguin approached Grapevine, but found she, too, was suffering from the virus that had attacked the other employees. As a result, she was feeling none too cooperative. Penguin decided that this was the time to test his plan. "I know this is a lot to ask of you, Grapevine, but without you we simply cannot succeed. You are the only one who can accomplish this mighty task." Hearing Penguin's words of praise, Grapevine bloomed with happiness, and she quickly set out to prove him correct. Within minutes his message had been delivered to every employee of Leaves-of-Wonderland. Penguin's job was done. Now all he had to do was wait to see how Alice and Beaver did with their assignments.

***

Alice, having received a promise from Duchess and Magpie, was on to the next department head who she thought might be willing to assist her—Puppy. True, Puppy had a difficult time paying attention, and was prone to making a mess of things, but Alice figured this was only because he had never had the training that he needed. His unbridled enthusiasm could be turned into an asset if she could only harness his energy. In addition, she had bet he hadn't been invited to the tea party because dogs don't drink tea.

As she entered the manufacturing department, Alice noticed that Puppy was still running from one end of the building to the other while his employees tried to stay out of harm's way. She watched the tableau for a few seconds, then placing her hands on her hips, she bravely stepped out into Puppy's path. She yelled at the top of her lungs so that the huge canine could hear her, "PUPPPY SIT!" and much to her surprise, he did just that. "Good boy," she said in her normal voice. Puppy wagged his tail, happy to have pleased Alice. "Puppy, lie down," she commanded so that the two of them would be at eye level. "You are such a good boy!" she praised him, patting his nose. "Puppy, I need your help."

With this Puppy let out a high pitched, excited woof. The only thing he liked better than being praised was being needed. "Very good, Puppy. Now I need you to listen carefully." The huge pooch put his head on the floor between his paws. "Puppy, do you know I am Alice, founder of Leaves-of-Wonderland?"

Puppy gave an excited yip of affirmation, then raised his enormous right paw as though to shake her hand. "Good boy, Puppy!" Alice happily exclaimed. "What I need you to do is to bring all of your employees to the clearing in one hour. Do you understand, Puppy?"

He looked at the clock that hung over the door, and then back at Alice, giving her a bark of understanding. "It is very important that you not be late. I'm counting on you," she continued. Puppy was so excited to be able to please her that he was having a difficult time staying put. Finally, Alice reached into her pocket and pulled out a large bone, and handed it to him. "Thank you Puppy for your cooperation. It means a lot to me. I look forward to working closely with you. You can go now." With that the big dog rose and emitted an exuberant bark, sending fearful employees running for cover.

Alice left the department with the satisfaction of knowing she had done everything she could, but she still felt uncertain of Puppy's ability to perform the task without her being there to give him commands. All she could do now was wait to see how he did.

***

While Alice had been visiting with Puppy, and Penguin had been getting out the message about the gathering through Grapevine, Beaver had been busy looking for Caterpillar. With any luck, the former would find the latter, and prevail upon him to help ensure that all employees were at the gathering.

Caterpillar, as a consultant hadn't been invited to Hatter's tea since he wasn't an employee. As a keen observer, he was aware of the goings on, and had simply puffed on his hookah as each of the employees who had drunk the tea lost all memory of Alice. Caterpillar didn't approve of management's methods being that they relied on deception, but it wasn't his place to condemn Hatter directly. That task must fall on Alice's shoulders, and he wasn't all too sure the girl was up to the task.

Beaver found Caterpillar dreamily puffing away. It took several attempts by Beaver to get his attention. "What is it you want?" inquired Caterpillar a bit testy at having his silent contemplation interrupted.

"I am here on behalf of Alice," responded Beaver in a loud voice so that he could be clearly heard by Caterpillar.

The consultant's irritation at the interruption dissipated, and he carefully crawled off his perch so that he and Beaver could speak. "Alice sent you?" he inquired with great interest. "What does she want of me?"

Beaver began to convey the tale of the events at the tea party, but Caterpillar impatiently waved the explanation away. "Yes, yes, yes, I know all that."

"Yet, you know who Alice is?" the confused Beaver inquired.

"Of course I do. I am a consultant. A good consultant. And, let me assure you that a *very* good consultant is aware of the ridiculous lengths that fools, such as Hatter, attempt in order to gain control of a company."

"Alice plans to fight Hatter and the Queen," stated Beaver firmly. "That's why I am here."

"Bravo for Alice," Caterpillar exclaimed with gusto. "It is high time she wakes up and take charge. I am proud of her for taking this big step and fighting for her business. What does she need from me? I want to be helpful."

Beaver conveyed Alice's message to Caterpillar asking him to come to the clearing to affirm her story and to assist her with the antidote. A frown creased Caterpillar's brow as he listened to Beaver. "She doesn't want me to blow smoke does she? Because that wouldn't be right."

"Of course she doesn't want you to blow smoke!" responded Beaver testily. "The antidote to Hatter's tea is the truth. Alice only wants you to affirm the truth when she shares it with everyone."

Caterpillar ignored the hint of impatience. With a smile that looked a great deal like pride, Caterpillar assured Beaver he would indeed be in the clearing at the appointed time.

***

Alice's final task was to talk with her legal team. While they weren't legal eagles, they were the best she had. "Maybe," she thought, "they will finally have the ability to leave the bar where they have been stuck for so long if they are given a challenge along with the responsibility and authority to help fix a problem." She was confident that they would not be feeling the effects of Hatter's tainted tea because they never were never convinced of anything unless it was attested to by a legal document and accompanied with evidence.

Alice entered Eagles Nest and saw her legal team of Griffin and Mock Turtle bellied up to the bar, right where she'd left them earlier. Griffin was the first to see Alice and said, "You can't be here!" Then realizing who he was addressing, he adjusted his tone and continued, albeit quite impertinently. "Oh, it's you again. What do you want?"

Alice wished she could say that what she wanted was for them to get off their seats, get to work, and show some respect, but she realized they needed assistance to get unstuck just as she needed help to accomplish her mission. So taking a deep breath, she replied, "What I want is your help."

After incredulously looking at one another and then back at Alice, they quickly jumped from off their stools, each firing questions at her in rapid succession: "Do you want to sue someone?"

"Do you want us to prepare an injunction?"

"We love to go to court unless, of course, it's the Queen's court."

"Do you want to order someone to cease and desist?"

"Shall we write a brief brief?"

"Are you the party of the first part?"

Finally, they both took a deep breath, and said in unison, "Well, speak up. How can we help you?"

Alice smiled at Griffon and then at Mock Turtle. She thought to herself, "At least they are enthusiastic, if not altogether competent. Perhaps with the right guidance these two might turn out to be fine employees." Then she addressed the pair. "There have been certain lies that have been spread about me."

"Slander!" exclaimed the zealous Griffin.

"Libel!" cried Mock Turtle with equal zeal.

"Yes, that is correct." Alice giggled, but quickly became serious again. "I need your assistance to help stop the lies."

"Of course you do," said Griffin, puffing out his chest with attitude.

"You require an injunction issued to the party of the second part demanding that such vilification cease forthwith," offered Mock Turtle in concurrence with his colleague.

"Yes, yes, yes! That is all well and good, but what I need immediately is your sworn testimonies before the assembled employees of Leaves-of-Wonderland stating for a fact that I am Alice, founder and CEO of the company. Can you do that for me?"

After some grumbling, huffing, and pontificating, the two would-be attorneys agreed they could and would help Alice. After giving them finalized instructions, Alice was once again on her way. It was time to reconvene with Penguin and Beaver.

***

With all their tasks completed, the three rendezvoused in Leaves-of-Wonderland Clearing. All they could do now was wait to see what happened. They hadn't long to wait, for at the appointed time, the clearing began to fill with employees. As Alice and her companions looked out over the crowd, they saw that everyone both great and small was present—from the tiny Cricket who worked in shipping, to the extremely large Elephant who worked in strategic planning. At the edge of the clearing in a tall tree, Alice saw the telltale smile of Cheshire Cat. At the front of the crowd was Caterpillar who seemed to just appear out of thin air along with his toadstool. Sitting on her kitchen chair was Duchess, still reveling in the satisfaction she was feeling as a result of Alice's recognition of her importance. The legal team of Griffin and Mock Turtle were perched on a log, carefully scrutinizing the assembly. Puppy was there too, sitting like a good dog, his tail wagging gently in anticipation. All of his employees were gathered around him, praying he wouldn't roll over and squish any of them.

WORKBOOK
15 GATHERING STEAM

SUMMARY

Alice and her allies quickly mount a plan to undo the damage Hatter has caused: first, to rally the support of those who already know Alice, then, onward, to convince the others of Alice's flesh and blood existence and of her honorable fight for the company.

Alice heads toward Quality Control to try to turn the Duchess in her favor, knowing full well that the Duchess probably had a hand in creating the dangerous tea Hatter had served to the staff. Alice is able to convince Duchess that she has her best interest in mind and respects and appreciates what the older woman has done for the company. Alice's sincere praise turns the stalwart quality control department head into a comrade ready to support the CEO's efforts.

Alice then visits her HR soldier, the squawking Magpie and quickly gains her second ally. With that accomplished, Alice sets out to see Puppy in manufacturing. The big baby canine is only too happy to obey her instructions.

Finally, Alice confronts the legal team explaining about the lies that Hatter has been spreading about her, and that she needs their help and sworn testimony to combat those lies. Despite their initial grumbling, the passionate legal force gets behind Alice, ready for a long awaited legal battle.

Meanwhile, Penguin is hard at work creating an employee event. He tells Grapevine to spread the word that a party is being given to reward and recognize employees. He assures her that this couldn't happen without her direct assistance. Grapevine is flattered and agrees to aid Alice's trusted assistant.

Beaver visits Caterpillar explaining that Alice needs him as an ally in her fight to take back rightful control of Leaves-of-Wonderland. Caterpillar is intrigued and happily surprised by Beaver's information, and wholeheartedly agrees to stand by the 'new' Alice at the upcoming gathering.

With their purposes fulfilled, our three friends meet at the appointed venue for the employee gathering. Before long, the crowd starts to form. Alice awaits her big moment to address them.

WHAT ALICE LEARNED

- A clear direction and plan with many pieces is necessary when a large goal is at stake.

- Alice, Penguin and Beaver need to communicate in the language of each of their potential allies in order to be understood and to be listened to. They also must keep the best interest of each ally in mind and address it in order to motivate them.

- She must accept there are many things beyond her control.

   What other lessons do you see that Alice has encountered in this chapter?

   _____
   _____
   _____
   _____
   _____
   _____

DISCUSSION QUESTIONS:

1. In this chapter, all of the employees, the team approached, are persuaded to follow. What would have happened if any one of them had not? Which of those approached would have been least likely to follow the plan? What could they have done to show their lack of support?

2. Why do you feel the employees were eager to show up to the Town Hall meeting in the Clearing?

3. How else could Alice have foiled Hatter's and the Queen of Hearts' plans to weaken Alice's influence and sell the company? What would you have suggested?

SHORT ANSWER QUESTIONS

1. How does Alice exhibit courage in this chapter?

   Why do you feel this way?

2. Do you feel there is a real leader or the key influencer other than Alice in the story?

If so, who? Why?

3. The **biggest** mistake Alice made so far in our story is:

   a. Not to have taken Cheshire Cat's warnings seriously from the beginning

   b. Not to have overseen Hatter's management of the company

   c. To have been entirely absent from the company for so many years

   d. Not to have taken herself seriously as a leader and as an adult with responsibilities

   e. Not to have been clear with Hatter as to his responsibilities when she hired him

   f. Not to have had a clear exit plan when she left the company originally

   g. To have hired a consultant and not to have listened to him

   h. Other

16 LEAVES OF TRUTH SERUM

As the small group of friends stood and watched, the clearing filled with Leaves-of-Wonderland's employees. There was much chattering, chirping, buzzing and squawking, about what this get together could mean. While Grapevine had been fruitful in spreading the news, she hadn't quite been able to keep the story straight about why everyone was invited to the big event.

Some employees were told they were going to be honored for their contributions to the company, others had been told there was some big cheese they were invited to meet – although who would want to meet a cheese wasn't quite clear. There were some employees who had heard there was news that the company was in hot water. Given the nature of the business, those employees weren't certain if this was good news or not. Still other employees didn't want to miss out on any good gossip, and that was all the encouragement they needed to attend.

At the back of the crowd, was Hatter. Seated next to him was the Queen of Hearts herself.

Alice took a deep breath and stepped out in front of the assembled employees, awaiting her formal introduction to the crowd.

There were a hundred butterflies trying to convince her to retreat and give up. They fluttered in her tummy, reminding her none of this would be happening if she had just minded her own business. Surely, Hatter and the Queen would not have held so many cards had she had only been a better leader. Alice shook her head, quickly quelling the troublesome butterflies. She knew she couldn't change what had passed; she must focus on the here and now so the future could be bright.

After what seemed to be an eternity to Alice, Penguin waddled out into view to announce Alice and to begin the meeting. He stood on a large rock ledge, serving as a platform. He began to speak in his typically quiet voice, and no one paid him the slightest attention.

"Speak up, Penguin," urged Beaver.

Penguin cleared his throat and began again. This time a few members of the audience closest to the ledge heard him and turned to shush those behind them. Puppy, saw Penguin was having difficulty gaining the attention he needed, and rose up and bounded to the front of the clearing, giving a mighty woof. This drew the attention of everyone in the crowd. Satisfied with the results, Puppy wagged his enormous tail and lay down at the base of the ledge.

"Thank you, Puppy," said Penguin, feeling a little disconcerted by the sudden attention that was thrust upon him. "I think you all know who I am, but perhaps you are unfamiliar with my position here at Leaves-of-Wonderland. I am the assistant to the CEO and founder of the company—Alice."

A murmur went through the crowd like a wave. Seeing Penguin was again in need of some assistance, Puppy emitted a low growl from deep within his throat. The audience quickly grew quiet, not wanting to arouse the dog's ire. Penguin continued. "I realize we have been told Alice does not exist, but I know otherwise! Alice is here and she asked me to introduce her. So, without further ado, I give you Alice, CEO and founder of Leaves-of-Wonderland."

Penguin, clapping his flippers with enthusiasm, turned toward Alice. There was a smattering of applause from the audience, but not enough to make Alice feel welcome. Clearly, this wasn't going to be easy. From the back, near Hatter, someone shouted, "I don't believe in Alice! I don't believe in Alice!" Soon another voice joined in, "I don't believe in Alice! I don't believe in Alice." Before one could say 'flibbertigibbet', the entire crowd was chanting, "I don't believe in Alice! I don't believe in Alice!"

Hatter and the Queen were smirking most unattractively. They smugly sat with their arms crossed looking as though they had won a major victory against their mutual enemy.

Caterpillar, perched as he was on his toadstool, puffed on his hookah, and listened to the crowd. The friends had predicted something such as this might happen, and so Beaver had given him instructions on what to do. Caterpillar was known far and wide for his excellent smoke rings, but few creatures knew of his other talent with the hookah. So, you can imagine the surprise of those gathered when they saw the enormous puff of smoke he emitted, which slowly formed into the letter "Q". The crowd was even more astonished to see a second letter emerge from Caterpillar. They pointed to the sky as a "U" appeared. More and more members of the audience became aware that something important was happening, and the chanting slowly died as they awaited the next letter. An "I" appeared followed by an "E" and then finally a "T". By this time the entire crowd was quiet.

"Now that I have your attention," began Caterpillar, "let me assure you Alice is as real as you and I. I can personally vouch for her as I've known her since she was a mere child, even before she gathered the original team together to start this tea company. I am proud to have worked with her for many years. So, you need to sit quietly and listen to what she has to say. You might learn something."

"Why should we believe you? You are nothing but a consultant! Hatter told us Alice is only a fairytale created to sell our wonderful teas, nothing more," yelled someone from the rear of the crowd.

"If she is real, why have we never seen her?"

"Not only have I seen her, I know her and I am happy to know her!" called out Duchess in her booming voice. There was a loud gasp from the crowd followed by a murmur. "QUIET!" she yelled. She waited for the gasping to subside before continuing. "We all drank Hatter's tea, and that is what made us forget Alice. Frankly, she wasn't much to forget…that is, until lately. Now you need to sit there, be quiet, and listen to our founder! That's more like it." Duchess said as the crowd fell into a stunned silence. She then settled her large form back into her seat, giving a nod of her head to Alice who had been waiting her cue to begin.

"I am Alice," she stated firmly, although her body was shaking with excitement. Once again the crowd became abuzz, so Puppy growled and everyone settled back down. "I know you have many doubts, and I certainly can't blame you. I haven't exactly been present lately. But I *am* the founder and CEO of Leaves-of-Wonderland."

"Prove it," demanded someone who sounded a lot like Hatter.

"Very well. If I may have the legal team of Griffin and Mock Turtle come forward."

Alice stepped aside as the almost-attorneys at law strutted to the center of the makeshift stage. Both stood very straight, a frown creasing their brows. They peered down at the crowd, trying for all their worth to look as official as they could. After clearing their throats several times, they each opened a large tome and began to read.

"Alice, heretofore known as the party of the first part, is, in fact, the founder of Leaves-of-Wonderland, hereafter known as the 'Company' as specified under Article 1, subparagraph B, part 5 of the Articles of Incorporation," declared Griffin.

"The party of the first part is also the Chief Executive Officer, hereafter known as CEO, of the Company per Article 12, subparagraph D, part 3 of the Articles of Incorporation," said Mock Turtle, picking up right where Griffin had left off.

"Yes," shouted the mysterious Hatter-like voice, "but how do we know this is really *the* Alice?"

"Do you doubt us?" demanded Mock Turtle.

"We are sworn officers of the court," exclaimed Griffin.

"Veracity is our hallmark!" declared Mock Turtle, feeling as though his character was being maligned.

"To be sure!" pronounced the other half of the lawyerly duo.

Hearing no further heckling from the crowd, the lawyers walked off the platform, leaving Alice alone to confront her employees.

"As I was saying, I am the CEO and Founder of Leaves-of-Wonderland. I may not have been acting as a leader should. No, let me rephrase that: I *have not* been behaving as a leader should. For that, I apologize to each of you. You deserve better, and I intend to see that you get better—starting immediately."

Once again, a murmur washed over the crowd. High up in the trees on the far side of the clearing, Alice could see the smile had formed into a huge grin. Evidently, Cheshire Cat liked what he was hearing. This emboldened Alice as she continued to address the assembly. "As you may or may not know, there is pressure from outside the company to force us to sell to a foreign entity. One potential buyer has been selling teas with names and packaging similar to ours. By doing this, they have been tricking our customers into thinking we are selling inferior teas. This is to make us vulnerable and more agreeable to sell." Alice caught the sight of Duchess' maddened expression from out of the corner of her eye. Clearly these were fighting words to the woman who took so much pride in the quality of the teas and who would not take this affront lying down. Alice knew she would have a loyal ally backing her, and that gave her renewed courage.

"I freely admit I am to blame for this situation. However," she paused for dramatic effect, "I intend to do everything in my power to prevent it. I cannot guarantee I can halt the wheels that are in motion, but I am going to do everything to ensure Leaves-of-Wonderland not only survives but thrives."

Somewhere in the crowd someone bellowed, "If you are really Alice, why should we trust you are going to start caring now?"

Alice swallowed the lump in her throat, knowing the person in the crowd had made a valid point. Why, it seemed like just a blink of an eye earlier when Alice resented her peace and quiet being interrupted by bothersome company issues. She hated to admit it, but she was the last one in the company to realize she was hurting Leaves-of-Wonderland, its employees, its customers, and even herself.

"Frankly, you cannot know until I have proven to you by my actions that I mean what I say. I have already started to work with the department leaders. Next, all of us need to start working together to make things better. Additionally, I want to meet with you, to learn more about what you do, and how we may be able to assist you in your jobs."

A tiny voice in front of Alice asked, "What do you mean?"

"I mean, that Magpie in HR has tried time and again to help by providing training and other assistance, but the poor thing's chirps have fallen on deaf ears. Her department has been ignored or, worse yet, used to feather someone else's selfish nest. That isn't good for the employees or for Leaves-of-Wonderland. But we are going to change that, aren't we Magpie?" she asked the bird who had joined Caterpillar atop his toadstool.

"Yes we are!" declared Magpie proudly.

"Additionally," continued Alice, waving to Magpie to join her on the platform, "I realize each of you have put forth so much effort without the leadership you deserve. I want to give you a token of my gratitude in recognition for your loyalty while I've been absent. Magpie will help me distribute the medals as I call your names." Taking her place beside Alice, the bird took a medal out of a box and flew to the first employee whose name Alice read. "White Rabbit."

After each employee had received a medal, and the tone of the meeting was on a more pleasant note, Alice said, "There is one more piece of business." Everyone quieted down, wondering what else she would have to say. "Hatter and the Queen of Hearts have also been a great help, and I want to recognize them."

A buzz went through the assembly which had nothing to do with the bees in the nearby trees. Alice let the din continue for a minute before she added. "I will be working very closely with both Hatter and the Queen over the next few months. Together, I believe we can bring this company back to full strength."

Alice stood on the ledge in amazement as cheers arose. There was a cacophony of happy cheers, whistles, and chirps—her employees were genuinely happy! She allowed herself a few minutes of well-being before bringing quiet back to the crowd. "This isn't going to be easy, but I know we can do it. I'm asking you to please give me another chance even if I don't really deserve it. Help me make Leaves-of-Wonderland great. Help *us* make Leaves-of-Wonderland great!" Once again, a rousing cheer arose and Alice felt her cheeks blush.

As calm descended, she saw that Hatter and the Queen were coming through the crowd toward her, both looking quite unhappy. Alice felt a moment of panic. The one part of the plan that was most uncertain was dealing with her two nemeses. Fortunately, Penguin had been able to provide information that would allow her to address each of their interests in a manner she hoped would inspire them to want to work with her rather than against her. This was her chance to give it a try.

"Please help me to welcome Hatter and our board chairman, the Queen of Hearts." The audience politely applauded as the two mounted the ledge and approached Alice.

"Thank you for joining me here," she told them. Alice knew she had just one opportunity to start this on the right foot. If, for some reason, she began on the left foot, all might be lost. Thus, she carefully chose her words. Penguin's intelligence work had let them know it was the Queen who had started all the trouble. Evidently, she wanted to have more control, but even more importantly, she wanted to be recognized as important, something Alice had failed to do. Consequently, as the Queen became increasingly angry, she caused quite a tempest in a teapot. This might easily have blown over, but Hatter had seen it as an opportunity to manipulate her by playing to her ego. They formed an uneasy alliance wherein both of them got what they wanted. Now, Alice needed to bring them back into the fold.

Firing Hatter was out of the question. Her board, led by the Queen, was deep in the game and they would never allow Hatter's termination, no matter how Alice might shuffle the deck. Thus, now was the time to lay all her cards on the table and hope for the best.

"Hatter and the Queen both have talents we need. Therefore, I am asking them to help me to make Leaves-of-Wonderland the best tea company in the world. For example, the Queen is the best at building empires, so, I will call on her to assist in mapping out our future. Hatter knows how to understand all the double-talk that is so common in business, is accustomed to organizing parties, and it's plainly obvious he is passionate about our tea. So, let's hear a round of applause for the Queen and Hatter." Alice motioned for them to come stand with her.

When the pair were there, next to her, Alice extended her hand first to the Queen and then to Hatter. Each wore a slightly dazed look as they took her extended hand in turn. However, as the applause and cheers in the audience increased, the two looked more and more pleased with themselves. Before long, Hatter had his hat in hand, waving it to the crowd. The Queen used her scepter as though she were knighting the employees. Off to the side, Beaver and Penguin exhaled a mighty sigh of relief. "Whew!"

At the end of the gathering, the employees collected together in small groups, dotted all around the clearing, to discuss the proceedings. Alice stood apart watching them, looking for signs that would give her insight about what they were thinking. What she saw and heard gave her hope, but her travels through Leaves-of-Wonderland had shown her that the employees had never really been a problem. They just needed a caring leader and they would be fine.

When Beaver and Penguin joined Alice, they were surprised to see a frown creasing her forehead. "You don't look very happy," said Penguin. "Isn't this the outcome we had hoped for?"

"Of course it is, dear friend, and I could never have done it without you and Beaver," she replied.

"Then why aren't you happy?"

"Penguin, I am happy with what we have been able to do thus far."

"Yet you look worried." Beaver interjected.

Alice sighed and said, "I'm very worried."

"But why?" demanded Penguin. "Everything went so well. Why are you worried?"

"Because now I have to put my words into action. This is all so new to me. I'm just not confident I can do everything I promised, and I don't want to let everyone down. They are counting on me. I asked for a second chance, now I have to earn the trust they have given to me."

The three stood together in silence, each in deep thought. Finally, Alice shook off her doldrums, put a smile on her face and said, "Well, one thing is certain: I won't get it done standing around here."

"Right oh! Let's get to work. What do you want us to do first?" asked Beaver.

"Don't look now," Penguin interrupted, "but our friends have their heads together. What do you suppose they are conspiring about?"

Alice's face turned a shade paler when she saw Hatter and the Queen glancing her way. "Oh, they are looking over here. I wish I was half as certain as I pretended to be up on that platform. If I were, I would march right up to them and confront them. Is there any chance they will go along with my plan?" she asked, looking for signs of hope in her friends' eyes.

"There is really only one way to know," answered Beaver.

WORKBOOK
16 LEAVES OF TRUTH SERUM

SUMMARY

As the employees gather, there is much speculation about the purpose of the meeting. Grapevine had done a fine job bringing the people to the clearing at the appointed time. However, as is her nature, there was a lot of confusion about the purpose.

When Hatter and the Queen of Hearts enter the clearing, Penguin's feathers become ruffled. As a testament to how much our heroine has grown, she assures Penguin it is good they are there because she, unlike them, intends to take the high road. Additionally, it is important the treacherous duo know the employees have learned the truth.

Alice is true to her word as she tells her story, conveying her culpability in the current condition of the company. With this truth serum administered, the effects of Hatter's tea begin to dissipate, but there is still much she has to answer for, and she doesn't back down.

With Magpie's assistance, Alice rewards each of the employees with a medal as a way to recognize their faithfulness to Leaves-of-Wonderland teas. Her final act is to introduce Hatter and the Queen of Hearts, much to everyone's surprise, most especially the two conspirators. She thanks them for their service and tells the assembly how they will be positioned to help her turn the company around. The crowd cheers, happy to see this apparently harmonious front focused on keeping Leaves-of-Wonderland Teas alive and well.

When at last the assembly begins to disperse, Alice confesses she wishes she felt half as confident as she had pretended to be. As she watches Hatter and the Queen, she wonders if they will go along with her plan. Beaver suggests there is only one way to know for sure…

WHAT ALICE LEARNED:

- Sometimes faking confidence will help you feel confident.

- Courage isn't a lack of fear; it is doing that which scares you in spite of the fear.

- Give someone a good name to live up to and they will seldom disappoint you.

    What other lessons do you see Alice has encountered in this chapter?

    _____
    _____
    _____
    _____
    _____
    _____

DISCUSSION QUESTIONS

1. This is the first time Alice has addressed the entire company as its leader and founder. What was the one incident in the story that enabled her to get to this point?

2. Were you surprised by the turnaround of Hatter and the Queen of Hearts? Why? Do you believe they will follow Alice? Was Alice was right to bring them into the fold?

3. Picture yourself as one of the employees who is not in a leadership role. As you listen to Alice, what would you have felt after the presentation? Would she have won your loyalty? Is there something more you wish she had said?

SHORT-ANSWER QUESTIONS:

1. Do you feel confident Alice can deliver on what she promised the employees?

   ___ Yes   ___ No

   Why or why not?

2. Who do you think will be Alice's **greatest** ally going forward: (Select best answer)

   a. Beaver
   b. Penguin
   c. Hatter
   d. Queen of Hearts
   e. Duchess
   a. Puppy
   b. Magpie

   Why did you pick this individual?

3. What should Alice's next step be? (Circle best answer)

   a. Meet with Hatter and the Queen
   b. Meet with the foreign competitor
   c. Discover who is the spy within the company
   d. Determine everyone's role in the turnaround of the company
   e. Meet with each department individually to get their ideas behind a potential turnaround
   f. Write a business plan
   g. Go to Disneyland
   h. Have a strategy session with Beaver and Caterpillar

   Why did you select this answer?

17 THE END, THE BEGINNING AND THE MIDDLE

Having become a true leader, Alice needed to know what Hatter and the Queen of Hearts were thinking. Were they with her or not? Did they have any more tricks under their hats? Could they work together given their history?

Feeling proud of herself, Alice realized her journey through Leaves-of-Wonderland had given her the confidence to approach them together…something that would have terrified her not so long ago.

Hatter and the Queen had their heads together in whispered conversation. As she neared, they stepped away from one another.

What would that discussion look like? What was in store for Alice as she was attempting to climb out of the rabbit hole? As the last remnants of slumber began to lift, the sleeping CEO fought to remain asleep a little longer. How could Alice help her? She was desperate to get some clues.

And then it was all gone…

There was a strong fragrance of nectarine blossom drifting through the air. It was fruity and sweet combined with a hint of fresh grass, carnations, and vetiver. The sweetness kept winding its way to her nostrils. She was aware of the scent at the same time she was aware she was shaking some kind of daze from her head. Within that daze, there was something about a big gathering—some form of meeting crossing her vision. There were a lot of characters involved. They were coming to some form of agreement however the future outcome was uncertain. The lingering thought captivated her, but she didn't know where it came from. In her last foggy moment, she tried to grasp at the details. She knew it might offer her some kind of sage wisdom there somewhere. She kept her eyes closed savoring the last remnants of the scene. It had been a triumph. R.S. desperately wanted to remember what that felt like. It had been a long time since she had experienced a triumph. Lately, it felt like a continuous uphill battle, and it was draining her energy and spirit.

Alas, it was a memory seen through a veil. She tried to make one last effort to reach it, but it slipped away. Picking her head slowly up from her desk, she shook it into alertness and brushed her hair out of her face with her hand. She felt a slight indentation on her forehead, probably left from the papers piled on her desk she had been trying to get through before she had fallen asleep.

Her tea cup, half full, was sitting next to the papers. Of course, it would be cold by now. She would have to warm it or make another cup. It was her favorite, Alice's Woods. She only allowed herself to drink it when rewarding herself. It was so expensive and difficult to find. Tonight's reward was due because she had spent all night, well, most of it anyway, trying to get through paperwork to resolve the issues her business was facing.

She looked around her office. The sun was shining through the office windows. It was around 7 a.m. she guessed, at least according to the position of the rays on her desk. In a few minutes she would have to close the shades in order not to be blinded by direct sunlight, but meanwhile she liked the way the sun felt on her face. It gave her hope.

R.S. looked at the cases of glasses along one wall. The glasses inside were perched on displays. They were of all different colors, textures, shapes, and sizes. Some of the frames were filled with sample lenses, some were not. There were those with dark lenses for the sun and some with colored lenses for the fashion conscious. No matter, mornings like this one, they all looked the same to her. They all had the same logo on them: *LookingGlasses*.

R.S. relished the quiet of her office as she gathered her thoughts on what to do next. The silence was going to be short-lived, however, as it was broken abruptly by a loud ring from her phone. "It's started already" she sighed. "No rest for the weary."

She picked up the phone and the voice that came out was loud, raspy, and quite startling for an early morning. R.S. held the phone out in front of her, afraid to put it to her ear.

"Rebecca Sue, what have you figured out? Have you gone through the papers? Where does the company stand? Do I have to call a board meeting?" It was the demanding voice of Regina Corazon, the Chairman of the board. No one else dared call her by her full name. She was always just R.S.

It was too early to deal with the barking Ms. Corazon, but R.S. had picked up the phone, and the no-nonsense woman at the other end would expect some kind of response. R.S. quickly mumbled, "Still going through the details, Regina. I'll get back to you." She then hung up, but not before hearing, "We can't wait all day. You'll have to get back to me soon or I will have to start chopping heads..."

Regina's voice was cut off.

R.S. smiled. She liked putting that egotistical woman in her place, even if it only meant hanging up on her mid-sentence. Yes, there was a board, but R.S. was still the founder of the company, the CEO, and the majority shareholder. Regina could only do so much damage.

Okay, what to do? Her first move, she ventured, was to call on the legal team and finance department to hear what they had accomplished toward assessing the situation of the business and her status within it. She was about to ring the attorneys, when her dapper assistant, Tuck Humboldt, walked into her office, his usual bowtie and jacket looking perfect. She smiled, recollecting some piece of her dream. Tuck reminded her of a loyal ally who had appeared in the dream several times. She felt good about his presence as a harbinger of better times ahead.

"Geesh, R.S., you made it here before me again this morning! This is not a good sign."

"Tuck, it's an important time for us. I need to be prepared for every possibility. There's so much to catch up on. It's almost overwhelming."

"What can I do to help, R.S.? Do you want a rundown of all the departments? Do you want me to call anyone? Can I get you coffee? Order breakfast?"

R.S. smiled at the generosity of her assistant. He was always willing to pitch in and help. He was so caring and dependable.

"Tuck, I had the strangest dream last night." The assistant cocked his head and looked at her. "I can't really remember the entirety of it, but the main thing was the message I learned from the dream: we can't give up." Her usual passion was beginning to reappear.

Tuck felt himself being swept up by R.S.'s mounting rush of enthusiasm as she proclaimed, "We have to move forward! So, let me tell you what I'm thinking. The first thing we need to do is…"

WORKBOOK
17 THE END, THE BEGINNING, AND THE MIDDLE

SUMMARY

There's a turn of events. There's a whole new cast of characters. Is this the same tale? Is this the same book? But, yes! We traveled through the world of make-believe creatures and with the rub of the eyes we encounter a world that is straining for change, like Alice's world, but feels more real, more like....

R.S., Rebecca Sue, wakes from a troubled sleep into the morning sun of her office. She has been at work all night trying to considering ways to get her business, LookingGlasses, out of trouble and away from a possible acquisition target. Where's the future of a small eyeglass manufacturer in today's world? She has been dreaming of a fictional company with a young woman at the helm. The CEO believes the dream holds lessons for her and her predicament if only she can hold onto the details of it all. RS tries not to listen to the self-doubt that lingers from the past and the remonstrance from her Board and focuses instead on the present. The dream has left indelible footprints on her brain and in her spirit.

RS's assistant, Tuck Humboldt, arrives at his office surprised to find his boss still at her desk. This is not a good sign. RS does not seem discouraged however. Instead, she seems to have found new strength, optimism and energy from a dream which she can't quite recall. She recounts to him the message she has received from the dream. A dream driving his boss to a new beginning? Must have been some dream! Yet, surely there have been stranger things that have happened in the past few months. Tuck begins to have a shred of hope they can turn things around at LookingGlasses. R.S. attempts to try to put her vision into words: "The first thing we need to do is...."

WHAT RS LEARNED

- Big ideas can come from the most unusual places.

- Dwelling in the past will not solve today's problems.

- The first step in solving problems is a belief they can be solved.

What other lessons do you see RS has encountered in this chapter?

_____
_____
_____
_____
_____
_____

DISCUSSION QUESTIONS:

1. What are the similarities between RS and Alice? How about their companies?

2. RS mentions that it has been a long time since she has felt like a winner. How does a sense of defeat impact your ability to solve problems?

3. We don't know much yet about RS' situation. However, knowing what you have learned about Alice and Leaves-of-Wonderland and the team she assembled around her, how would you suggest RS assemble her team of allies? What attributes should be represented?

SHORT-ANSWER QUESTIONS

1. RS uses her favorite tea to reward herself. How do you reward yourself for a job well done or as motivation for a hard task?

2. Do you feel RS having spent the entire night in the office has improved her chances of coming up with a solution to her problems? Or would she have been better off leaving and coming back? What have you found works best for you?

3. If you were Regina Corazon how would you have reacted to RS' handling of this morning's phone call?

WORKBOOK
18 *YOUR* STORY

SUMMARY

This chapter is strictly for your own personal usage. Alice's story has been told…at least to a point. What about yours? You've read the book. You've completed the primer. Now it's time for you to move on - just like LookingGlasses and Alice's tea company. Use this space to write down what you want to remember and keep with you as you move forward in your life. You can take it with you!

Lessons you encountered while experiencing Leadership in Wonderland:

_____
_____
_____
_____
_____
_____
_____
_____
_____
_____
_____
_____
_____
_____

What are the things you most likely will remember about reading the book?

How will those things you learned impact your personal journey as a leader going forward?

How will you implement what you've learned?

Leadership in Wonderland

How will you measure your success?

How will you celebrate your successes?

Alice had Beaver and Caterpillar as her mentors/advisors, and Penguin as her 'cheerleader' on her journey. Who do you have or could you have to assist you?

ACKNOWLEDGEMENTS

We would like to offer our thanks and hugs to all who have helped to make *Leadership in Wonderland* a reality.

- ★ Lewis Carroll for introducing us to Alice and Wonderland.
- ★ Our beta readers – Amanda, Stanley, Dave, Margaret, Maisha, Carol, Karen, Albert, Larry, David, Maryanne, Melissa – who shared their wisdom and insights.
- ★ People who embraced our Alice fixation: Beth and Paul, Susan's parents, Shelley and Sandy, and Rebecca's cousin, Cheryl.
- ★ All the characters we've encountered in our work (Alice, Beaver, White Rabbit, etc). You know who you are. (Willie Nelson, too)
- ★ Larry Lacy who misdialed.
- ★ David Gabor who introduced us and LinkedIn that made it possible.
- ★ Countless friends and family members who have listened to us talk about this book and supported and encouraged us enthusiastically to get it finished and published.
- ★ Our pets – Blu, Ziggy, Chewie, Corkie, Fly and Miss Kitty – who patiently waited for walks, meals and attention while keeping us company during long hours of work.
- ★ The Rabbit Hole – we've all been down it.
- ★ Rebecca's writers' groups, the 750 Writers Group and Parkland Writers Circle, who inspired, encouraged and helped us navigate the publishing waters.
- ★ Tea – you helped make this project a party and inspired Leaves-of-Wonderland. We'd also like to thank, in advance, the companies that want to create teas inspired by our book. We look forward to drinking them.
- ★ Alice fans who have helped to keep her alive.
- ★ Sir John Tenniel, the artist in the original Alice's Adventures in Wonderland, whose drawing graces the cover of our book.
- ★ Our clients who have taught us so much.
- ★ Rob Tozer who edited the manuscript for us with such precision. You rock!!

- ★ Cees Talma for encouraging us to continue by sending a selection of tea.
- ★ Kathy at Get a Book Deal who offered us great advice.
- ★ The kind people who shared sample proposals.
- ★ Lauren Galit of LKG agency, who gave us the title. Without you, the book might still be called The Wonderland Odyssey.
- ★ All the writers who came before us who wrote books that inspired us to be different.
- ★ SKYPE, what would we have done without you? Our phone bills would have been astronomical!
- ★ The people who we forgot to thank. This will save us from having to smack our forehead when we remember.

Thank you all!

Susan and Rebecca

ABOUT THE AUTHORS

Susan Goldberg is a specialist in hiring and coaching young senior professionals and those who hire them in the media and technology industries. She has been working with leaders to gain the right footing and climb out of their particular rabbit hole of finding and retaining great people since the 1990's. She also writes and speaks on these topics. This book was an idea that sprang from an article she wrote for a New York newsletter on business lessons learned from reading the original Lewis Carroll classic.

Susan's continual passion for life and work comes from learning and looking at things from an unexpected view. She is inspired by an entourage of mentors with varying degrees of education and experience. Those sources of wisdom are professors, classmates, advisors, trainers, friends, family, authors, journalists, clients, and kids.

Susan comes from a long line of entrepreneurs on both sides of her family. Therefore, it was inevitable that after receiving a bachelor's degree in French Literature from Washington University in St. Louis and an MBA from Pace University, along with years as a marketing manager and then search consultant, that she would become a business owner. Her company, Susan Goldberg Executive Search Consulting, works with media, technology and digital marketing companies to find and keep their most valuable young senior talent.

Susan lives and works in New York with her collection of eyeglasses and her dog, Blu.

Rebecca Lacy will be the first to tell you she is Alice. She has experienced self-doubt and the hurdles of becoming a leader similar to what Alice encounters in Leadership in Wonderland. Because there's a little Alice in all of us, Rebecca helps clients find their own path to become successful, confident leaders. She has coached and trained members of the clergy, non-profit leaders, medical professionals, small business owners, students, artists, volunteer leaders, as well as government and corporate employees. One thing Rebecca has learned from her clients is that one-size never fits everyone, thus, her interest in creating Leadership in Wonderland to help readers discover their inner leader.

Rebecca also feels life is much too short for work not to be enjoyable and feeling good about your skills goes a long way to making that a reality. Learning those skills is easier when you actually get pleasure from the process.

Rebecca, who holds an MBA in Business Management, is president of Pinnacle Management Group, a company that provides training, coaching, and assessments in the areas of team engagement and leadership development. Rebecca is active in the arts and works with several not-for-profits in her community, and is a columnist for Women's Voices Magazine.

Rebecca lives in Farmington, Missouri with her husband, Larry, and their menagerie of furry and feathered friends.

To learn more, about the authors and to download the fillable forms, visit **http://www.leadershipinwonderland.com.**

You can also follow them on:
http://www.facebook.com/leadershipinwonderland and
http://www.twitter.com/@LIWAlice.

Made in the USA
Middletown, DE
27 October 2016